W9-BKE-055

$\mathcal{H}$ASH

A NOVEL

TORGNY LINDGREN

Translated from the Swedish by Tom Geddes

OVERLOOK DUCKWORTH
Woodstock • New York • London

First published in the United States in 2004 by
The Overlook Press, Peter Mayer Publishers, Inc.
Woodstock & New York

WOODSTOCK:
One Overlook Drive
Woodstock, NY 12498
www.overlookpress.com
[for individual orders, bulk and special sales, contact our Woodstock office]

NEW YORK:
141 Wooster Street
New York, NY 10012

Originally published in Swedish as *Pölsan* by Norstedts Förlag, Stockholm,
Sweden, in 2002.

The publishers gratefully acknowledge the assistance of the Swedish Institute
toward the translation of this book into English.

Grateful acknowledgment is made to Random House, Inc. for permission
to reprint an excerpt from "The Eighth Elegy" of Rainer Maria Rilke's
Duino Elegies from *The Selected Poetry of Rainer Maria Rilke*,
translated by Stephen Mitchell © 1980, 1981, 1982 by Stephen Mitchell.

⊗ The paper used in this book meets the requirements for paper
permanence as described in the ANSI Z39.48-1992 standard.

Library of Congress Cataloging-in-Publication Data

Lindgren, Torgny, 1938–
Hash : a novel / Torgny Lindgren ; translated by Tom Geddes.
[Pölsan. English]
p. cm.
I. Lindgren, Torgny. II. Title.
PT9876.22.I445 P6413 2004   839.73—dc22   2003063976

Book design and type formatting by Bernard Schleifer
Manufactured in the United States of America
FIRST EDITION
ISBN 1-58567-408-7
1 3 5 7 9 8 6 4 2

And we: spectators, always, everywhere,
turned toward the world of objects, never outward.
It fills us. We arrange it. It breaks down.
We rearrange it, then break down ourselves.

—RAINER MARIA RILKE

I

HE WAS STANDING at his writing-desk. It was Monday the twenty-second of December nineteen hundred and forty-seven, the snow already so deep that nothing more could happen in the district, absolutely nothing. No one could drive on the roads, no milk had been delivered to the dairy for several days, the trains were at a standstill in Bastuträsk. He had just heard the weather forecast: a cold northerly airstream was sweeping across most of Sweden. A fresh to strong north-northwesterly wind bringing snow squalls and colder temperatures was heading down over inland areas of Norrland. Temperatures between minus thirty and minus forty Celsius could be expected overnight.

He was writing a local news report. He had started it on Saturday. It was a good piece. On the radio Nanna Lundh-Eriksson was talking about the eighteenth-century early feminist poet Hedvig Charlotta Nordenflycht. There was a smell of stewing meat in the kitchen where he stood, of allspice and bay leaves and cloves. His article was growing by several words a minute, and it might turn out quite long.

MYSTERIOUS MAN

There are persistent rumors that a recently arrived traveler in the district, a middle-aged man with a German-sounding name, is not the person he purports to be. Although he speaks Swedish with hardly a trace of accent, and although he seems to have adapted readily to our climate and our way of life, his whole demeanor has something transient and foreign about it. He has unobtrusively taken up residence in a remote farmhouse outside Avabäck belonging to Mrs. Matilda Holmström, a widow who moved away to Adakgruvan after the death of her husband to take up employment as a cook. The house is in a state of disrepair, but the kitchen and bedroom are said to be habitable.

Neighbors passing by in the evenings have heard the new occupant singing, in a strong and melodious voice. The local cantor, Mr. Landkvist, summoned to give an opinion, recognized the stranger's singing as including several arias by the German composer Wagner. An opera by the same composer, *The Twilight of the Gods*, has recently been broadcast on the radio. The orchestra was conducted by Wilhelm Furtwängler. One of the roles was sung by the Norwegian soprano Kirsten Flagstad.

> **Avabäck.** Village 14 miles northwest of Vormforsen in the Vindelälven valley on the border of Västerbotten and Lapland. Situated in predominantly unproductive land. Cultivated area ca 20 hectares, mostly drained marshland. 23 inhabitants. Sights: ruins of a small bldg by Avabäck River, possibly a watermill.

AS HE WROTE, it stopped snowing and darkness was already descending. The kitchen clock struck three. The talk on Hedvig Charlotta Nordenflycht had come to an end, and now there was a gap in programs until five o'clock, when there would be a performance by the Radio Chamber Orchestra. He could easily expand this report to a hundred lines, with no trouble at all:

The widespread rumors in circulation locally over the last few days conjecture that the musical stranger near Avabäck may actually be none other than

JUST AS HE reached this point in his narrative the door suddenly opened and from outside in the darkness his mail was flung in and landed on the kitchen floor. So someone must have made his way down to the village and fetched the mail that the bus had gotten through with. Two of last week's newspapers, Christmas cards from his cousins in Boden and his eldest sister, the one who was a cleaner at the school in Boliden. And a letter from the editor.

He rinsed his hands in the bowl on the washstand before sitting down at the kitchen table and with some solemnity taking the carving knife to open the letter. Never before had he received a communication from the newspaper's editor.

"It pains me considerably," he read, "to have to write this letter. I hope you will find it equally painful reading.

"Our newspaper has always regarded its primary task as disseminating information and facts. Our news and reporting, even our advertisements, must be in absolute accord with reality. Our readers must be able to open their newspaper with a feeling of trust and confidence. A good journalist is one who seeks the truth with dignity and rigor and seriousness of purpose. His material is the self-evident and irrefutable. His prime responsibility is to suppress his own personality in the interest of objective truth, authentic and verifiable.

"For some time now, after tactful inquiries from perplexed and concerned readers, we have carried out careful investigations into the veracity of the reports you have submitted over the course of the years, the all too many years, which we have published conscientiously honestly and fearlessly.

"Having done so, we have found your reports, not to put too fine a point on it, completely devoid of any basis in fact. The reality which you appear to describe is nothing more than a figment of your imagination.

"The dramatic week-long struggle to rescue an elk from Höbäck marsh never took place. The schoolhouse in Avaberg that burned down three years ago never existed. No unknown celestial body 'with shimmering corona' ever rose above your horizon. There has never been a turkey farm ravaged by a bear in your district. Nor has there ever been a factory producing vitamin shampoo. I could go on.

"The individuals whose births, birthdays, marriages, and in some cases even deaths, you have reported, have never lived on this earth. On further reflection, it seems remarkable to me, not to say quite extraordinary, that you yourself actually exist.

"The villages in which you have made your characters live and die are nowhere to be found; these villages which patently seem to lie within our circulation area are not on any map. Let me just name Avaberg, Inreliden, Risträskstrand and Lillåberg. We commissioned the District Surveyor, Mr. Cederblom, to search the land registry, and he confirms that none of these places is recorded, not even in variant spellings.

"In summary: you are a fraud. A liar and a forger. A swindler and a rogue.

"Yet I shall not presume to sit in judgment upon you. Not upon you personally. It is my conviction that at the root of all our thoughts, notions and metaphors there are hidden motives, pretexts and urges over which we have no control. This must apply *ipso facto* to the countless reports you have invented. The whole affair therefore is best left as a matter between you and Our Lord. We shall likewise refrain from demanding reimbursement of the over-generous per-line fees we have paid you over the course of the years. Despite the fact that we would undoubtedly have the law on our side.

"One inviolable precept, indeed an eternal commandment, is that *mere invention and fabrication and idle imaginings shall never under any circumstances find their way into print.*

"Reality is by its very nature documentary.

"I therefore *impose an absolute ban* on your writing reports henceforth. *I forbid you to write another word!*"

He read the letter twice. Then he sat still for a long time with his hands clasped in front of him. His wife had boned the meat and was now at the sink feeding it through the mincer. The intermission on the radio was over and the gramophone record of the day was Feodor Chaliapin singing "La calumnia e un venticello" from Rossini's *Barber of Seville*. On the Decca label. It was followed by the Vienna Philharmonic playing the slow second movement from Schubert's *Symphony in C Minor*.

He was fifty-three years old. What else could he do?

In the end he went across and picked up the writing-stand—it had been made for him by Elon Persson from Lillåberg—and carried it into the pantry with his notepad and other paraphernalia and put it all next to the wall shelf where they used to keep the cream separator. He would not write any more.

At least, he declared to his pencil and the sloping top of the writing-stand, at least not for a good while.

Yes. It would certainly be a good while.

2

HE COULDN'T STOP thinking about the response he would have written to the editor had it been allowed; the thought preyed on him disproportionately. This prohibited letter occupied his mind day and night, at times as brief as an announcement of the death of a baby, but some days and especially some nights expanding mercilessly: it could have filled the Christmas Eve special reading supplement. For Christmas 1938, for example, he had written eight hundred and sixty words about venerable Christmas traditions in Lillåberg. There were days when he envisaged the letter in large-font letters, even underlinings and exclamation marks, not to mention subheadings; on other days the forbidden and thus non-existent text shrank almost to invisibility, small, secretive signs imbued with acuity and irony. When he stood at the window watching the crows wheeling or the rafts of logs floating downstream across the lake it was the end of May, and the ice had melted. His right hand moved in the air as if he were writing.

Occasionally on a summer evening he would go out into the forest, up to Klåvaberg hill, where he would sit on a tree-trunk and speak the unwritten. Speaking was permitted. He would talk to the mosquitoes and the lemmings and the vixen, who presumably had cubs in a den on the hillside leading down to Gårdmyren marsh. His words mingled with the scents of the flowering lingonberry bushes and the turpentine of the pine trees.

It is easy, he formulated the unwritten and unwritable, it is so easy and so comfortable being editor and just sitting in a brick house down on the coast sending off impudent letters upcountry. An editor can always write effortlessly, of course, writing flows from an editor just like any other bodily fluid. Whereas someone who writes without any position in society, in a small wooden cottage, line by line, as it were, has to force his words up and out from much deeper observation, he has to choose words with the utmost care because he has no choice, he writes from an awareness and a perception and a seriousness of purpose which is unknown in the towns of the coast.

You seem to think that my news and other reports are products of my imagination and of my desire for income-generating fantasies. You contrast imagination with truth as if the two were incompatible, as if they were mutually exclusive, as if imagination were not a product of reality. You write about truth as if it were yet another of your possessions, as if it were at your personal disposal in the same way as the PHOTOGRAVURE DEPARTMENT, the COMPOSITING ROOM or the PRINTING PRESS. To put it bluntly: you have not understood the essential nature of truth. Allow me to quote the great philosopher Bernhard Bolzano:

"Truth in itself has no real existence, that is to say it is not anything which exists as real in any particular place or at any particular time or in any other specific way. Admittedly both known and merely imagined truths have a real existence for a limited time in the consciousness of the thinking or knowing person. They exist as particular thoughts which arise at one particular moment in time and cease at another. But we cannot ascribe any existence to the truths themselves that provide the material for these thoughts, that is, the truths in themselves."

I must mention in passing that Bolzano suffered from pulmonary tuberculosis and lost his professorial post in Prague partly because of the truism I have quoted. If he had written reports for your paper he would likewise have been dismissed.

A newspaper is a spiritual enterprise. All things spiritual are individual and dynamic, they are living organisms, they are both consciousness itself and the objects of consciousness. The essence of spirit is having itself as its own object. The spirit exists, according to Kierkegaard, as a dream within man. To have responsibility for a newspaper is to have responsibility for the spiritual, the profoundly human.

I have an image before me of how you take that responsibility: flaccidly and comfortably slumped in a soft armchair in front of a highly polished desk, you write down the words that flit through your erratic and irresolute head. You have, if I am correctly informed, inherited your position and your fortune and your newspaper, you have never needed to exert yourself. Even your hunched posture is an inheritance. You write in exactly the same way as you sit.

You know nothing of the courage and pride that a person writing from his innermost soul has to summon. And maintain. For his own sake. And for the outside world.

I write standing up, standing to attention, you might say. I do not even support myself against the writing-desk, I never rest my lower arm on its sloping top, I let my hand flow freely and unaided. That writing-desk was made to my own specifications by Elon Persson, the carpenter in Lillåberg. He was struck down by tuberculosis two years ago. You will find the obituary I wrote about him in the last issue of March, 1946. He was one of my people.

It is for the sake of these people that I write, the people whose existence you refute. Yes, I write for the whole region that has been entrusted to me. It is a duty I cannot repudiate, to defend Avaberg, Inreliden, Lillholmträsk, Lillåberg, and all the other places for which I am responsible. It could be said, of course, that my reports emanate from a desolation, not to say desert, which is unendurable, lacking as it does both sidewalks and store windows. But this happens to be my calling, and it is my opinion that your heavy-footed local correspondents in Medle, Rönnskär, and Ostvik are no match for my skill and artistic flair and aptitude.

Finally I must mention two reports that were about to have been submitted if your letter had not so cruelly and peremptorily terminated the flow of my pen in mid-stroke, so to speak, reports which have in fact been in progress for some time already.

The first concerns a stranger who arrived unexpectedly in the district, and has apparently taken up residence in one of the abandoned farmhouses that tuberculosis, or death in general, has produced or discarded. His presence is enveloped in rumor and hearsay, enough to provide material for a dozen more articles.

The other report was to have dealt with the galloping spread of tuberculosis, now raging in Avaberg, and to describe its progress. The illness is called *phthisis florida* in Latin. Its victims quickly develop a pallor. In the course of a week or so both lungs degenerate into a bloody paste. The epidemic has already carried off four local boys and girls. Their obituaries would have appeared as appendices to the main piece.

Apart from these two items I had already drafted about twenty lines on the current shortage of schoolteachers.

This and much more will not now be available to your paper. I just wanted to let you know.

BUT THAT LETTER remained unwritten, as did any other. He wrote it, but at the same time he did not write it. He put it off for a future occasion.

No, he wrote nothing. Not even his name. He invented an identity sign for himself. It was the severed paw of a squirrel. Many years before he had translated a verse by Rückert:

> *In the life that came before*
> *to be a squirrel was my fate.*
> *In Eden there'll be Grace in store*
> *when I regain my squirrel's shape.*

He used that mark when he signed the agreement with the Holmsund Company for the sale of his forest. He used it too on the tax assessment forms that Edvard Holmgren in Gårdskläppen completed for him. Edvard Holmgren had a wooden leg and a clipped mustache. Sometimes in the spring he used to go out across the snow on his kick-sled to hunt the mating grouse. But the hinge of his wooden knee-joint cracked like a detonator with every step he took and scared off all the birds for miles around. He worked for the Internal Revenue.

THE MARK OF the severed squirrel paw was also to be seen here and there on barn walls, dried cowhides, chamois leather gloves, milk pails and fishing gear. But never his written name.

IN HIS LETTER to the editor he would also have liked to quote Goethe: "So both children and adults are wont to transform the noble and the sublime into a game, even into buffoonery how else could they bear or endure it?"

3

IN A WRITTEN account events seem actually to take place. But is there really any connection between events and the writing that describes them? Is the writing itself an event? Or is it manifold events, compressed into tiny squiggles, often black on a white background? Do events occur at all in reality, events with a beginning and an end? Or are they created in writing, with sentences, paragraphs and chapters that is, as a result of the written word's need for order and method?

He was standing at his writing-desk again after all.

So what had happened?

THE EVENT THAT had taken place was a very simple and straightforward one: the newspaper editor had died. He had fallen asleep at the age of ninety-eight years, five months and six days, at home, surrounded by his nearest and dearest, which is to say his grandchildren and their children and their dog Snuff, a poodle. The funeral would be a private family affair. Those who wished to honor the memory of the deceased were requested to remit an appropriate sum to the Newspaper Publishers Association Fund for the Freedom of Speech. He was a luminary who would never be forgotten. One of the greatest editors of his time. Our former editor would be awakened on Judgment Day by the Lord God Himself.

So his death had lifted the prohibition on writing.

That was why he was standing there again with his pen in his hand, on the seventh of April in the year two thousand. His posture was very upright, perhaps even a little stiff, and he was squinting against the spring light streaming in through the Venetian blinds. He had put on his white shirt and black pants, and had dug out a tie from one of the cardboard boxes under the bed, a blue one with red stars and polka dots.

HE HAD READ of the death two days ago in the newspaper. He had not been expecting it. But he had taken it into account as a possibility. Age is a tough adversary. Most people eventually have to admit defeat.

He had immediately asked the social services people to fetch his stand-up desk.

"Carry her carefully," he had said. "She was made by hand in Lillåberg more than seventy years ago. She's in the pantry by the table where we used to keep the separator. It's impossible to place a value on her."

She, of course, was his writing-stand.

And his spiral-bound notebook was still lying there exactly as he had left it more than fifty years before. The sharpened pencil was tucked down inside the spiral wire. Only the unwritten stood between him and his notebook.

He had no choice, he had to continue where he had been interrupted by the editor's letter.

HE HAD BEEN living in Sunnybank Rest Home for nineteen years. He had his own room, just as the Liberal Party had promised in the Seventies. He had his meals served on the table next to his armchair. Someone brought him a sleeping pill every evening. The doctor had offered him a tranquilizer, but he had rejected it. He was given a shower twice a week. Once every two weeks a podiatrist came to trim his toenails, scrape the soles of his feet with a pumice stone and rub aromatic oils between his toes. Three care assistants took turns to make his bed. They were pretty and kind, and he felt very close to them. A cleaner came to vacuum the floor every other day. From time to time a nurse would monitor his very low blood pressure. Seven years earlier His Majesty the King had sent him a telegram on his hundredth birthday. He got all the books and magazines he could wish for from the local public library. Occasionally the minister looked in on him. Every month he ordered two bottles of brandy through the manageress. A physiotherapist checked once in a while that he was doing various beneficial exercises.

In brief: he was being cared for like any other senior citizen. He had no objection to that at all. But he did refuse to wear a diaper.

WITHOUT WRITING, time simply flows by. If anyone had asked him what he had been doing all these years, what had been happening to him, he would have answered that he didn't know. He would see when and if he wrote about it.

He had survived his old age, that was all he knew for sure. Most people succumb to it. He had not.

In Avaträsk there had been a wall clock that one of his forebears, Erik Johansson, had made in the 1830s. It was called the Gransjö clock and had only one hand, the hour hand. In September 1944 this single hand had come loose on its spindle and stopped on six o'clock. But the clock itself, the original clock, continued to work. And that was the main thing.

One of his great-grandfather's sisters had survived old age and come out the other side at the age of a hundred and five. But then she had gotten too lively and had gone back relentlessly through her mature years and middle age and youth in the course of just a couple of years, before self-indulgently reverting to childhood and fondling kittens and dolls, until finally, sucking her thumb, she had regressed to the unborn fetal state. She, Sara Vilhelmina, was a warning to all.

He would have to be on his guard.

How could he be sure he had really survived his old age?

The times he had lived through had not been given written form. And old age leaves no wounds or scars.

No, he had no proof. But he had his convictions. Most proofs are no match for a conviction. The closest comparison to anyone who survives old age is a marathon runner who never needs to reach the finish or a ski-jumper who is never forced to land.

Year by year his skin was becoming smoother. And like Goethe, he woke with an erection every morning. Death was receding further and further from him. Two new wisdom teeth had emerged in his upper jaw. He was once more able to hum Peterson-Berger's arrangement of Fröding's *Titania*, even the difficult passage conveying the rustle of hazel and birch. His hair had started regrowing on the nape of his neck and at the temples, dark and thick. The podiatrist heaped praise on his feet, no corns any more and the nails increasingly strong and firm. Even his sight had improved: he was reading the newspaper without spectacles, including everything that had been written about the former editor. When he raised the Venetian blinds he could see hare tracks in the fresh snow on the hillside up towards Noret. His knee joints and lower vertebrae no longer ached. Some nights he could even sleep without pills. The flesh was filling out his cheeks and wrists. His navel was deeper. Swedish hash had started to taste almost as it had in his youth, even Holmlund's factory-produced stuff. He had started sweating again the way he used to.

If he had had to compose an article on the subject, he would have written: Everything seems to indicate that the old man has not just lived through his old age but has also survived it. Our paper will follow his progress with interest. Readers will be kept informed.

Yet up to now everything had by and large remained unwritten. He had counted the years: fifty-three. Years are not at all the same as events. And not all events are describable or even possible to substantiate. Some events are embedded in the dark void between cause and effect, they seem not actually to have taken place. Other events are as sudden and astonishing as the interference and breaks in the television transmissions from the Olympic Games in Munich. But nobody remembers them afterwards. Some events turn out to have happened without anyone noticing them. They become visible, as it were, only in the traces and effects they leave behind. If even there. He felt no anxiety or fear of the unwritten as he stood there at his writing-desk.

He would write for his readers.

Everyone who writes, writes for a readership.

As an experiment, to try out his hand and the pen and the daylight, he had written a few lines:

A writer needs well-worn, threadbare words. His world is simple but inexhaustible.

There was an immense amount that he must not forget or omit. Accidents, deaths, birthdays, lectures on abstinence, political meetings, unusual human-interest stories, weather observations from upcountry Västerbotten, exotic birds that had been sighted singing on a fence somewhere, splendid new buildings. Much of what time had arranged in a particular sequence would be mixed up and transposed, but that did not bother him. A degree of disorder and confusion seemed to correspond quite nicely with the timeless aspects of his own existence.

And his readership?

No writer can know anything for certain about his readership. Readership as a concept is one of those illusions which are intimately connected with the written word.

First and foremost there was probably Linda. She was one of the three who continued to look after him, despite the fact that it really was not necessary any more, and who thus shared his life. The other two were Niklas and Susanne. Perhaps the minister too belonged to his readership. And his podiatrist. Maybe also the folk-singer from Vindeln, who came once a month at the behest of the local council to sing songs by Evert Taube and Dan Andersson in what was called the day-room. And why not the ninety-year-old David Israelsson next door to him? Admittedly he was regarded as being on the brink of death, but one never knew. They used to exchange little greetings via the staff. One of them might ask, for instance, "do you remember Anton Sikström in Granbergsliden?" And the other would reply, "Yes, of course I remember him!"

Nothing is as unknowable and elusive as a writer's readership.

He must write his wife's obituary. When he found the right moment. It was twenty years now since she had died. But before that he would have to write the announcement of her seventieth birthday. He could also use that with some slight modification for her eightieth. In the obituary he would mention God and Eternity, maybe even Resurrection on the

Day of Judgment and the resumption of lifelong companionship. Even though at the moment that seemed unlikely, the way things were going.

But first of all he must return to the report he had just begun when the editorial edict had silenced him:

4

THE WAR CRIMINAL Martin Bormann, wanted throughout Europe, and even in South America. In the two years that have elapsed since the war there have been countless reported sightings of him: as a ski instructor in the Austrian Alps, on trains near Paris and Budapest, as a sailor on an Atlantic steamer, a baritone in a church choir in Jylland in Denmark. He has even been spotted attending a conference on nuclear disarmament in Amsterdam.

Now he has turned up here.

One afternoon in August this year he appeared quietly at Manfred and Eva Marklund's kitchen door in Avabäck, bowing politely. Eva was at home alone, since Manfred had been admitted to the sanitarium in Hällnäs a month or so before.

> **Martin Bormann.** German politician and war criminal. Condemned to death at Nuremberg for crimes against humanity. In 1942, realizing that the war would be lost, he engaged the services of a Swedish language teacher, Mrs. Elsa Richter, born in Linghem in Östergötland, widow of a German officer. From her learned fluent Swedish, with a slight regional accent. After the collapse of the Nazi regime, B. disappeared without a trace.

"I wonder," said Martin Bormann, "whether it might be possible to obtain a meal?"

"There's a guest house in the village," Eva Marklund replied.

"I know," said Martin Bormann, "I saw it as I drove by."

"But I could make you some sandwiches," she said. "If that would do."

"That would be fine," he said.

As she was buttering two thick slices of bread and cutting off some meat to put on them, he said, "My name is Robert Maser. I'm a refugee from war-torn Germany."

"I can tell you're not from around here," she said. "Would you prefer coffee or milk?"

"In the district where I was raised in Mecklenburg," he said, "we used to mix coffee and milk together."

Then he added, "Do I really not speak Swedish properly?"

"Well, you may," said Eva Marklund, "but I can tell you're not from around here."

She looked out of the window from time to time as she worked.

His vehicle was standing outside.

"Some jalopy you're driving," she said.

"Yes," Robert Maser admitted. "It's a special type of conveyance."

She told him to come over and sit at the table, pulling out one of the eight-rail chairs for him.

When he had poured both milk and coffee in his cup and taken the first bite of his sandwich, he looked up at her with his round, inquisitive face and asked, "What is this?"

"It's Swedish hash," she said. "Cold hash. When the hash is cold, it goes solid so you can cut it in slices."

"Hash," he repeated, his eyes fixed on the sandwich, "that's a word I've never come across."

"It's one of the most common words in the language," said Eva. She was sitting on the wood-box by the stove.

"It melts in the mouth," said Robert Maser. "In Mecklenburg we would call it potted meat. This Swedish hash is the most delicious potted meat I've tasted in my whole life."

"My hash," she said, "is pretty basic. There's hash that's far better. And there's hash that could be said to be supreme. And then there's even hash that can only be described as out of this world. But that's something we don't talk about."

When Robert had eaten the sandwiches and emptied his cup he put some coins on the side of the Christmas cactus saucer.

"It's getting cold," he said. "I'll have to find somewhere to stay."

"Yes," said Eva, "there are seven seasons here. One spring, one summer, one fall, and four winters."

"In Mecklenburg," he said, "we were never aware of more than four seasons."

"I've seen in the newspapers that people eat horsemeat in Germany. But it didn't say whether they stew it or roast it."

"Most people stew it," he said. "Then you mince the cooked meat to a brownish gray slop. And you eat it with a spoon."

"But I know of a house," she said. "It's empty. Matilda Holmström left the key with me. In case anyone might want it. It's nothing special. Just a house."

"A roof and four walls," he said, "is all I need. In Germany you often find three walls and half a roof. Or four walls and no roof. Or a roof with two walls."

"They've only got themselves to blame," she said.

"Yes," said Robert Maser. "They've only got themselves to blame."

"Though it's kind of hard to understand why you've made your way up to this neck of the woods," she said.

He didn't respond immediately. His eyes were roving around the kitchen. The wall clock showed nearly half past two. The kitchen stove was an Ankarsrum. There was a red and white striped hand-towel hanging from the key of the pantry door. There were already several buds on the Christmas cactus.

Eventually he said, "I've been looking for ages for a landscape that would match my state of mind."

She stood up and took a couple of logs out of the woodbox. As she pushed them into the stove, she said, "Yes, we should always be ashamed of what goes on inside us."

THEY WERE NO longer alone in the kitchen. While they had been talking a third person had crept in and sat himself on the stool by the door. He did not greet them, he did not remove his mottled gray cap, he just sat still and quiet watching Eva Marklund and Robert Maser. He had two sheath knives hanging from his belt, one against his left thigh, one against his right. He probably belonged to the house in some way.

So Eva Marklund fetched the key that Matilda

Holmström had left in her charge, the key to the empty house, and gave him careful directions. He shouldn't turn off towards Inreliden at the end of Höbäck Marsh, but just carry straight on. There would almost certainly be some logs in one of the sheds.

"That's only Bertil," she said about the young man by the door. "He pops up all over the place."

It was the afternoon of his second day, the second day of his resumption of writing. He had just formed the phrase "all over the place" when Linda arrived with the lunch tray. Pork sausage with potato and mashed turnip.

He was pleased with "all over the place."

It described not just the unpredictable Bertil with his sheath knives but also what he was writing.

"It's a fine phrase," he said to Linda. "All over the place."

"I much prefer order and method," said Linda.

"All over the place is also a kind of order," he pointed out. "Just different."

She looked at his notepad and the finished pages lying on the table.

"You mustn't work too hard," she said. "Exerting yourself won't do you any good."

"There's too much ginger in this sausage," he said. "And it's very lean. When you cut into pork sausage, the fat should spurt out of it."

And as she absently leafed through his sheets of paper he

told her about the pigs that had grown up during the time of Stalin and Churchill and Per Albin Hansson, about sausages white with fat, about sausage meat you kneaded with your hands that was so dripping with lard that you never had to wear gloves to protect your skin all the following winter.

5

But Robert Maser was not the first to visit Eva Marklund that fall. The schoolteacher, the new one, had arrived a few weeks earlier. He had already moved into the little apartment on the upper floor.

In all reportage the writer must ask himself: what should be mentioned first, and what second? Some events have to be narrated forwards, others backwards. How can we know what is really the beginning, and whether it is the effect or the cause? And what is the end, is it the cause or is it the effect?

Why had the twenty-eight-year-old schoolteacher Lars Högström found his way specifically to Avabäck?

In the summer of 1948 he had gone into town to see the Principal, having just qualified from the teacher training college in Umeå and seeking a post as grade school teacher. He could provide a health certificate as well as proof of residence.

"And what sort of thing did you have in mind?" the Principal asked.

"More or less anything," said Lars Högström. "Somewhere rural. A village school. I was born in Rönnmyrliden in Ångermanland. Something similar to Rönnmyrliden."

"Everything here is like Rönnmyrliden," said the Principal. "Apart from the main urban center the whole district is just marsh and pine forest and felled clearings. And tiny villages and isolated farmhouses."

He was smoking a cigarillo. The Hymnal and a couple of sheets of music lay in front of him on the desk. By leaning forward Lars Högström could see that it was Reger's *Passacaglia in D minor*. A few bars here and there were marked in red ink.

"Those are the difficult passages," the Principal said. "The color helps me focus my attention on it. I'm preparing the Sunday service. 'They that are whole need not a physician, but they that are sick.'"

He flicked the ash off his cigarillo and took a deep puff. The hymn book was open at "Lead us, heavenly Father, lead us."

"But you haven't any choirmaster's qualification, Mr. Högström?" he asked.

"Unfortunately not," Lars Högström admitted. "But I sing. Preferably duets. Quartets. Tenor."

"Reger was a schoolteacher too," said the Principal. "And he was in a sanitarium from time to time. But his vocal works are far superior to anything he composed for the organ."

"If I get a post here," said Lars Högström, "I'll read up as much as I can on Max Reger."

"Mind you, he's a bit overestimated," said the Principal. "He was essentially an eclectic. His variations were much too free. He was a Catholic trying to pretend he was orthodox."

"It doesn't pay to be false," said Lars Högström. "Falsity is always exposed in the long run. The only thing that gives life meaning is seeking the sublime and the sources of truth."

"And what may I ask is it that you're seeking?"

"Seeking," replied Lars Högström, the schoolteacher, "is putting it a bit strongly. But there is one natural phenomenon that particularly intrigues me. Which I would very much like to understand. Which for me is one of life's great mysteries. Pulmonary tuberculosis."

"Consumption," said the Principal.

"That's a word that sounds slightly vulgar," said Lars Högström. "In any formal context we say pulmonary tuberculosis."

Before the cigarillo burned his fingers the Principal stubbed it out in the ash tray modeled on the open-cast mine at Kristineberg. He was abstractedly whistling a passage of Reger out of the left corner of his mouth while pretending to read Lars Högström's transcripts from Umeå teacher training college.

"As far as consumption is concerned," he said eventually, "there's no better place than Avabäck. The teacher succumbed last spring. Everyone is infected. Or infectious. I haven't ventured there myself for five years. The District Inspector has never been there. When the women milk the cows they have to move their hands in time to the cows' coughing."

"I'll take it," said Lars Högström.

HOW DID LARS Högström come to have such an interest in consumption?

Even when he was taking his examinations in Umeå he had asked one of the proctors, a Mr. Falck, who had been born in Lillhärdal, whereabouts in Sweden the most virulent and concentrated tuberculosis was to be found.

"Here in the interior of Västerbotten, without a doubt," the teacher had replied. "One of my closest friends is chairman of the National Tuberculosis Association."

"And that applies to all forms of the disease, in all bodily organs?" Lars Högström asked.

"As far as I know," the teacher had replied. "Although pulmonary tuberculosis is the most frequent, of course. Lungs without cavities or spots or scars are pretty rare in upcountry Västerbotten."

"Well," Lars Högström had said, "it's also pulmonary tuberculosis that's closest to my heart."

HE WAS WEARING his best black graduation suit, clasping the certificate he had just received from Mr. Fahlgren, the Director. They were standing in the great entrance hall outside the main auditorium and he was alone with Mr. Falck, who was wearing a black jacket and striped pants. All around them small groups had formed of newly qualified teachers with their lecturers and examiners.

"But there are other types of organic tuberculosis that are at least as well worth considering," Mr. Falck was saying. "Less trivial. A shoemaker near Lillhärdal caught it in the testicles.

He went mad. He died in a strait-jacket in the sanitarium."

"Yes," said Lars Högström. "Tuberculosis is really fickle and unpredictable. You never quite know for sure where you are with it. But even pulmonary tuberculosis is a profoundly and distressingly grave matter, in my opinion."

"The brain can be affected too," Mr. Falck continued. "The results can be astonishing. Modernist poetry. Atonal music. Anarchic political programs. Non-figurative painting. But most common, of course, is pure and simple idiocy."

"One can but wonder," said Lars Högström, "whether there isn't some overall connection between tuberculosis and insanity."

"It wouldn't surprise me," said Falck. "I've heard that said about upcountry Västerbotten. Lots of the inhabitants end up in the sanitarium in Hällnäs. And there must be many more who are admitted to the asylum near Umeå."

It was early summer outside, beyond the high windows. Birds were feeding on the wing, butterflies wafted on the breeze, clouds of pollen drifted by.

"And how tuberculosis is spread is still a mystery," said Lars Högström. "I can't help thinking of concepts like fertilization and pollination and fecundity."

"Well, I suspect the mosquitoes," said Falck. "I was exposed to upcountry Västerbotten mosquitoes just the once. My car broke down in a village called Lillåberg.

> New teacher in Avabäck. **Lars Högström** has been appointed to the vacant teaching post, on a temporary basis.
>
> Högström is a recent graduate of the teacher training college in Umeå. Parents and pupils in Avabäck will be pleased to welcome a certified teacher to the school once more. Mr. Högström has been an enthusiastic duet and quartet singer during his time in Umeå.

There were more mosquitoes than air. There was no question of breathing, in any normal sense of the word."

"Not to mention all the other gnats, midges and horse-flies," Lars Högström added. "All the man-eating insects in the dikes and marshes."

"Under those circumstances I would have chosen a suitable sickness for myself," said Falck. "In fact, any sickness at all. Just to escape. Maybe even tuberculosis."

The schoolteachers and lecturers around them were beginning to move off towards the main stairs. Outside in the courtyard friends and relatives were waiting. The newly certified teachers were to be fêted with flowers and song. A brass band could be heard from over in the schoolyard or sports arena. It was playing the national anthem.

As they reached the top step Lars Högström asked, "What happened to his wife? The shoemaker's wife near Lillhärdal."

"Tuberculosis of the ovaries," Falck replied. "What else would you expect?"

One of the new teachers had evidently overheard their conversation. He remarked that the current inoculation program with Calmette vaccine would definitely eradicate tuberculosis from the face of the earth.

"That remains to be seen," said Lars Högström.

"It's been a great pleasure talking to you," said Mr. Falck as they arrived in the lower hall. I've enjoyed it."

"The pleasure has been all mine," Lars Högström replied.

"What did you say your name was?"

"Lars Högström," said Lars Högström. "From Rönn-myrliden in Ångermanland."

SO HOW HAD he come to this point, to the door through which the newly certified teachers would emerge, to the four years of teacher training, and before that to the preparatory course at college?

It was consumption that had brought him here.

The illness presented itself when he was eight years old. It had been uncompromisingly revealed by an x-ray examination. For the next five years he had been cared for at home, with only occasional periods at school.

In his fourteenth year, in March, he had finally been allocated a place as one of the hundred and twenty-eight patients at Österåsen Sanitarium. From his bed he had a view of the River Fax.

He was there for eight years. Sometimes the river was covered in ice, sometimes not. Other patients came and stayed for a while, then disappeared, some to die, some because they got well. The two kinds of disappearances seemed to be of equal value. Life was exactly as Thomas Mann had described it in *The Magic Mountain*.

BUT ONCE, ON a hot August day, he saw a motorcyclist down on the main road. The heat had been streaming up the river valley. The motorcyclist had his mouth open to the wind, his hair billowing out behind him. It was impossible to guess where he was going, and it looked as if he were laughing at the warm breeze rippling through him.

It was an unforgettable sight.

WHILE WAR RAGED in Europe, he studied, getting through all the high school subjects by correspondence course. He took the oral part of the examinations at the school in Härnösand.

One day a doctor came in and sat down at his bedside.

"Studying," said the doctor, "gives us a belief in the future."

"The future?" said Lars Högström.

"An active life," said the doctor. "When sickness and everything else has been overcome."

"If the future didn't exist," said the still ailing Lars Högström, "we wouldn't have to worry so much."

"As far as I'm concerned," said the doctor, "I believe in chemistry above all else. Virtually every question that Creation has left us to ponder can be answered by chemistry."

"I can't perform laboratory experiments," said Lars Högström. "Where you have to add one thing to another. And heat everything up to a hundred degrees. I have to believe in my correspondence course."

"The majority of experiments fail in reality," said the doctor. "It's the descriptions of the experiments that are always more credible and reliable."

"I imagine how everything is," said Lars Högström. "And imagination is also a kind of experiment."

"Indeed it is," the doctor replied. "There's no real distinction between imagination and faith."

This was the doctor who sometimes played the flute in the Christian Fellowship Group.

"Do you pray to God?" he asked.

"Who else should I pray to?" said Lars Högström.

Before the doctor left he laid a green apple on Lars Högström's bedside table.

A FEW DAYS into the new year of 1944 Lars Högström was called in to see the physician-in-charge.

"Happy New Year!" the doctor said. "Yes, even more than that: Happy New Life!"

"Excuse me?" said Lars Högström. "I don't get you."

He tried to cough. But he no longer could.

"You're cured," said the doctor. "Completely and definitively cured!"

"I don't understand," said Lars Högström. "It can't be possible."

He sat down on the hard, imitation leather patient's chair in front of the physician's desk. In his hand he held the pocket watch he had inherited from his father. It had become a habit for him to have the watch with him to check his pulse.

"Your sedimentation has stopped. Your x-rays show complete healing. No one could be healthier. We could sell your blood as a tonic."

"I sometimes feel a bit feverish," said Lars Högström.

"Imagination," the doctor retorted. "Nothing but imagination."

"Isn't there any way I could get sick again? Any remedy that would help?"

"It's a great privilege to be able to give people a clean bill of health," the doctor replied. "Anyone discharged has been through an extremely trying time. And has passed with flying colors."

"I've enjoyed it here," said Lars Högström. "And in a few months' time the river will be unfrozen again."

"Mr. Högström," said the doctor, "by the time the River Fax thaws, you will be a long way from here. You'll have come to grips with life again by then."

"I don't know what I shall do," said Lars Högström. "Isn't it possible there's been some mistake? A mix-up of case notes?"

"You're not merely healthy," the doctor said, "you're more than healthy. I'm not exaggerating if I say you could eat infectious matter by the bucketful. There aren't many people who could go out into the world with an immune system like yours."

Lars Högström looked at the watch he was holding. But it had not stopped. He put it in his pocket.

"I've got nowhere to go," he said. "I hadn't expected to be discharged just like this.

"And the food!" he added, his voice almost rising to a falsetto. "The whole sanitarium, all its corridors and stairs and lobbies, full of the constant smells of stewing and new-baked bread and cloves and oranges. Where in the world shall I be able to find such nourishing and well-cooked food?"

He was particularly fond of the potted pork with mashed turnip and potato and pickled gherkin or beetroot. And herring pie with melted butter.

But the doctor was adamant.

He usually recommended the newly discharged to take up an artistic career, preferably painting or literature. Tuberculosis, he thought, with its slightly elevated temperature and enhanced but at the same time rather diffuse sense of reality, often constituted the first, tentative steps as an artist. The main thing was that one should have something to strive for.

But that was absolutely nonsensical! The Högström family had never shown the slightest inclination or flair for art. In his own case, he, Lars Högström, was totally indifferent to art of any sort. No, he would despise himself if he stooped to any kind of artistic activity. If he really was compelled to find some occupation or career, then it would have to be a proper and honorable job!

The doctor had started looking through the pile of papers on the desk in front of him. Taking out a fountain pen from the inside pocket of his jacket and writing some words at the foot of one of the pages, he said, "Then there's nothing else for him but a teaching career.

"But even a teacher," he muttered as he went on writing, "can probably live a meaningful if modest life. More or less, anyway."

AND HOW HAD consumption once so long ago, to be precise twenty-one-and-a-half years before that first afternoon at Eva Marklund's kitchen table in Avabäck, found its way to him?

He was six years old, and it was one spring afternoon in Rönnmyrliden. His brothers and sisters and parents were working on the hay racks in the upper fields of the farm.

There was a strange cow, a little black and white cow he had never seen before, down by the road to Norrböle. She had come meandering out of the forest, a cow with a hot muzzle and unusually bright, feverish eyes. She may have belonged over in Tjärnbodarna. She was eating the new grass bordering the ditch.

She was not afraid when he went up to her. He crawled underneath her and took hold of one of her teats and squirted the warm sweet milk straight into his mouth.

That is how it happened.

6

IT WAS MOSTLY very quiet where he stood writing in Sunnybank Rest Home. But he had a little transistor radio to play himself music and also provide him with regular news bulletins. National wage negotiations had reached a critical phase. A volcano had erupted in Mexico. The Liberal Party was drafting its new manifesto. Baby, baby, can't you hear my heart beat? The Prime Minister was in Brussels. There might soon be peace in Jerusalem. No one should feel unwanted or alone. Toptwenty@radioswedendotcom.

He had noticed a little hole in his tie. It was an annoying blemish he could see every time he bent forward to insert a full stop or a comma.

While he was recounting the conversation between Lars Högström and the teacher, Niklas brought him his coffee and bun. An hour or two later, just as the physician-in-charge at Österåsen Sanitarium was pointing out that tuberculosis with its more diffuse sense of reality often presaged an artistic

career, Susanne served up pancake with diced pork and lingonberry sauce.

"Where's Linda?" he asked.

"She's sitting with Svea Dalberg," Susanne replied. "Svea
is dying. Someone has to be with her. Why do you ask about
Linda?"

"I like her," he said.

"When Svea is dead," said Susanne, "I'll tell her."

A QUARTER OF an hour after he wrote "That is how it happened," Linda came in. He was still standing at his desk reading what he had written. Should he explain for the benefit of
his readers that the lost cow was infected?

"Is Svea dead?" he asked.

"Yes," said Linda, "it's all over."

She sat down on his bed and caught up her heavy dark
hair in both hands and let it fall over her shoulders.

"Is your back okay from all that writing?" she asked.

"I don't write with my back," he said. "I write with my
memory."

Her eyes never wavered from his writing-stand and the
window and possibly the begonia that the manageress had
given him, her fingers playing with the amber beads of her
necklace, as he explained to her what memory really was. It
was a cavity within a person that can contain just about anything. Where the past blends with the non-past and what has
been with what is to come, where friends and strangers live
their carefree and somewhat diffuse lives together side by

side, where the clock hands have stopped though the clock is still going, where the ice freezes at the same time as it melts, where there are words but also many things for which no words exist, where there is much that is clearly written but also blurred indecipherable signs. Unforgotten sicknesses, followed by healing and aromatic birch leaves. And deep down, in the well of inexhaustible memory, is the divine mercy that has made everything happen and brought everything into existence, all the past and all that which has not happened or existed but which is nevertheless right and proper and has its place, everything that is held aloft by the almighty hand of Grace.

"Her children and grandchildren live in Södertälje," she said. "They weren't able to come."

She was still talking about Svea Dalberg.

"There's a hole in my tie," he said. "I can't understand it."

He took it off and handed it to her.

"You can't get these ready-knotted ties any more," she said. "Every man can tie a tie nowadays."

"I bought it from a German," he said. "A German who drove around in a bus selling clothes. That was a year or two after the war."

"But one of her daughters is

> **Svea Dalberg**, widow, has died at the age of 81. At the time of her decease she was a resident of Sunnybank Rest Home.
>
> In the 1940s and 1950s she and her husband ran the farm at Lillåstrand, and she was greatly respected as a dutiful and capable farmer's wife.
>
> From 1942 to 1944 she was chairwoman of the local group of the Liberal Democrats Women's Association.
>
> Her oil paintings of cows, sheep and goats from recent years have received wide acclaim. She is mourned by her children and grandchildren, all of Södertälje.

arranging the funeral," Linda said. "And the Dalbergs' house in Lillåstrand is already sold."

"He lived in Avabäck," he said. "And he used to drive everywhere in the summer in that bus. Though the suit I bought didn't stand up to the rain."

On the radio a male group was singing, "I would give everything I own, just to have you back again." Their voices were strangely delicate and feminine.

"Do you think you could mend that hole?" he asked.

"I can try," she said.

7

So THE NEW schoolteacher had sat in Eva Marklund's kitchen. "My name is Lars Högström," he had said. "I've been told this is the house the teacher usually stays in."

And she had explained everything to him: the rooms on the first floor had been the teacher's apartment for decades. A bedroom and a simple kitchen and a living room, and all with mansard ceilings. But the last teacher who lived there had had consumption, and it was probably still ensconced in the walls and ceilings and floors. She had burned the bedclothes and the curtains and scrubbed everything with soap and lye, but the contagion was cunning and hardy and stubborn: it had even made its way down the stairs to her husband, and now he was in the sanitarium in Hällnäs.

She had to admit that she herself had recently had a slight hacking cough; she had to warn him, out of compassion. It would be best if he found himself a room elsewhere. As far as she was concerned it was enough to have had the previous mortally ill schoolteacher to worry about.

She had put out some sweet rye bread and butter and a plate of sliced hash for him. He had begun by eating some bread, but soon he devoted his whole attention to the hash. He cut it up into little morsels which he let melt in his mouth, and leaned forward at intervals to sniff covetously at the chunks still lying on the plate. Each time he put a new piece on the fork he studied it at some length before placing it in his mouth, twisting and turning it as if he were trying to understand how it was constructed, how the various ingredients had been blended together into such a unique entity.

In fact Eva Marklund wanted to advise him not just against moving into the rooms on the first floor, into what was known as the teacher's apartment. No, for her peace of mind she had to warn him against taking up the post in the school as well. All the schoolchildren were infectious, to varying degrees but all just as inexorably, they all had an aunt or an uncle or brother or sister in the sanitarium at Hällnäs, they all had swollen glands or microscopic spots on their lungs or the beginnings of fluid in their little pleurae. Over and above that she had to tell him that there was no real health or salubrity anywhere in the whole region. The so-called vaccine had arrived too late, everything dead or alive had already been contaminated in one way or another. As soon as he had eaten his hash he ought to get away as fast as he could to a healthier and more flourishing area.

"Hash?" he said. "This is called hash?"

"Yes," she replied. "It's Avabäck hash."

"I've never tasted anything so delicious before," he said.

"Back home in Rönnmyrliden hash was a brownish-gray stodge that reeked of entrails."

ON THIS OCCASION too the youngish man with the two sheath knives had come creeping into the kitchen. He did not greet them, he kept his cap on, he sat himself down just inside the door, very carefully so the stool wouldn't creak. Every now and then he felt his cap with both hands to make sure the peak was perfectly centered above the tip of his nose. Lars Högström ignored him: he was still concentrating on the hash.

"It's not like anything else at all," he said. "Not sausage and not veal loaf or headcheese or meat roll or pigs' trotters. And certainly not like sausage meat."

"No," said Eva Marklund. "Of course not."

"It's absolutely unique," said Lars Högström. "It could conquer the world."

"Avabäck hash is more or less entirely meat," she said. "Maybe just the odd extra ingredient. But in Morken it's even stronger."

Yes, she went on, there were plenty of other types of hash, and they were all more remarkable and more complex than Avabäck hash. She should make special mention of Lillåberg hash, which was very finely minced and kind of smoother. Not to speak of Raggsjö hash, which was darker in color but light in taste and had an aroma reminiscent of ginger yet not exactly ginger. Any chance to eat that hash was a real privilege. And the hash in Amträsk had a tantalizing hint of juniper berries if you savored it on your tongue. But over and above all others was the hash in Lillsjöliden, Ellen's hash in Lillsjöliden. It wasn't just a village hash but an individual's hash. It was incomparable. Once you'd tasted that, everything else was no more than ersatz hash or makeshift hash. And it kept well, from one fall to the next, succulent and strong, fresh and sharp, with a flavor of all the various organs and body parts that had gone into it. People would walk miles for a single bite of it. Ellen in Lillsjöliden had to double-lock the cold-store where she kept it. During the hash-making days in October the smell of her cooking spread as far as Inreliden and Lillåberg, and folk went and stood out in their yards just to be able to breathe and sate themselves on the vapors and fragrances.

"You don't happen to have the recipe?" Lars Högström asked.

"Recipe?" said Eva Marklund. "A recipe like that wouldn't be possible. Who would be able to understand it? It could never be written down on paper, there's a limit to what words can describe!

"But," she went on, "I'm not one to complain. We must all be content with the hash we've been granted."

THEN SHE ASKED whether he was still intent on taking what was known as the teacher's apartment, after the dreadful and discouraging information she had given him about the previous schoolteacher. She didn't want to try to stop him in any way, no, as things stood with her at present she would be more than happy to have him up there above her, but he must go into it with his eyes open, he must be aware of what he was doing. A person should always go to meet his fate with as great a knowledge and understanding as he could possibly achieve. The previous schoolteacher's consumption had been of the feverish and hemorrhaging kind.

"Nothing in the world would prevent me from moving into those rooms," said Lars Högström.

Then he revealed his secret to her, as indeed to the man in the cap over by the door.

He was immune, and could never come to any harm.

And to be on the safe side, in case immunity was an unknown concept upcountry in Västerbotten, he explained its meaning in greater detail: the immune person was inviolable and invulnerable, immunity was a powerful force that acted as a protector and preserver and conserver, it was a shield and armor; immunity embraced its own and stood by them constantly and kept them unscathed. The immune individual could only be killed by the proverbial silver bullet. Here in Avabäck he had found his right place at the right time.

"The tuberculosis germs up there in those two rooms under the mansard roof," he said, "are going to get what's coming to them!"

It was also important to see immunity in a wider context. If immunity could be spread, more or less in the same way that sickness was spread, then masses of people could avoid their doom. The majority of people were susceptible, whereas only a few, far too few, were immune. So immunity had to be passed on to the susceptible. When you saw all the wretchedness and destitution in the world nowadays, and he would mention specifically the documentary movies he had often seen at the cinema in Umeå, then you couldn't help feeling a pain beyond words. It was fundamentally this lack of immunity that was the real evil and danger in the world today. He was certainly not immune to the suffering of others. What he was trying to describe was the blessing of immunity, not to say the gospel of immunity. And what she, Eva Marklund, his future landlady and hopefully future cook, what she had said about the suffering that had befallen not only her house but also the entire district, had affected him deeply.

"Suffering?" said Eva Marklund. "I never said anything about suffering!"

He had just put the final slice of hash in his mouth. He sucked on it thoughtfully.

"No," he said at last. "You didn't use that actual word."

"We're not suffering," she said. "We've never suffered. We know what suffering is, but it has never afflicted us. We endure. Most of the time we endure joyfully. Will one pillow be enough or do you want two?"

"One will be fine," he said. "If it's new down."

"THEN I'LL GO on upstairs and make your bed," she said. "And tidy things up."

"I like to sleep with my head under a half-open window," he said.

He had eventually had to swallow the last morsel of hash and surreptitiously licked the plate clean. Now, as she went upstairs to get everything ready for him, he could turn his attention to the man on the chair over by the porch door.

8

THERE WAS SOMETHING unusual about the appearance of this man. There was no one individual feature that was conspicuous, not his nose or neck nor either of his hands, nor the shape of his head or torso: it was the man in his entirety. But it was impossible to determine or describe what was strange or aberrant even in the whole.

"What's your name?" Lars Högström asked.

"Why do you want to know?" the man by the door responded.

"I'm Lars Högström," said Lars Högström.

"I know. I saw you arrive on the bus. And I saw you finding your way to this house. And it was obvious from your suitcase and your briefcase that you were a schoolteacher."

"So you followed me?"

"Of course."

"Were you thinking of helping me? If I got lost?"

"It's hard to lose yourself here in Avabäck. From the crossroads there's really only one way to go."

Eva Marklund came scurrying into the kitchen to fetch a chamber pot from the pantry.

"Oh, that's just Bertil," she said.

The chamber-pot was white enameled steel with a blue handle. She filled a pitcher from the water bucket by the sink.

"Have you tasted the hash in this house as well?" Lars Högström asked.

"Why do you ask?" said the man called Bertil.

As Eva Marklund leaned forward there was her slight hacking cough again.

"It's such excellent hash," said Lars Högström. "I've never enjoyed anything so much in my life."

"You're trying to get me to commit myself," said Bertil. "You're hoping I might say the wrong thing."

"I was only trying to make conversation," said Lars Högström. "It's quite natural for two people who find themselves sitting together in a kitchen out in the country to talk to one another. It doesn't have to mean anything special."

"You can't be too careful," said Bertil.

"No. Of course not."

"I think Avabäck hash is about average," said Bertil. "Neither better nor worse."

He was resting his elbows on his knees. The two sheath knives hung straight down from his belt. His lumberjacket was buttoned right up to the neck.

"The birch trees are turning gold already," said Lars Högström. "And the willowherbs are wilting. I presume fall comes extremely early upcountry. It's a different climate from down on the coast."

"Are you reporting back to the authorities?" asked Bertil. "Collecting information? Filling out forms?"

"Why should I be doing that?" Lars Högström replied. "I've come to teach children. That's all."

"We're always being watched," said Bertil. "We have to be on our guard."

"Why should the authorities be watching Avabäck?"

"I don't know how it is elsewhere," said Bertil, "but here in Avabäck we're under surveillance all the time."

At that moment a little gray tractor and trailer drove past outside.

"There was once a man here in the village who used to write about us in the newspaper," said Bertil. "We were never safe. But he's stopped."

The cat, which Lars Högström had not noticed before, jumped up onto the windowsill to look at the tractor.

"That's Simon," said Bertil. "He's bringing up the hay racks from down on the marsh."

"How do you know?" said Lars Högström.

"You should never relax your guard and get careless," said Bertil. "That can be the most dangerous thing of all."

Then Eva Marklund reappeared to say that the rooms were ready. "Perhaps you'd like to come and see if everything's more or less all right."

Bertil followed them. He stopped halfway up the stairs to hear Lars Högström say, "I haven't had anywhere so neat and nice and homely since I had to leave Österåsen Sanitarium."

9

"I'm AMAZED AT your energy," said Niklas, depositing the breakfast tray on the table.

"What do you mean?"

"Standing there writing day after day," said Niklas. "As if you were paid by the hour. As if you weren't free to do what you liked."

"I only compose one sentence at a time. When I've constructed a sentence I write it down. Have you ever thought about what a sentence actually is?"

"Do you want applesauce in your oatmeal?" Niklas inquired. "I can go fetch some."

"When you make a sentence, you're completely free. A sentence that is simply itself. Creating sentences is the highest and most dignified form of activity human beings can strive for. Many people live for eighty or ninety years without producing a single sentence."

"Your oatmeal is getting cold," said Niklas. "It'll go solid and inedible. And the milk is skinning over."

"You'll get older. You'll come to understand what sentences mean. There are occasions when a single sentence can protect us from annihilation. Would you like to try reading what I've written?"

"I read sometimes," said Niklas. "But to be honest I don't get any pleasure from it. It doesn't stick. I understand everything but don't have any use for it."

"No, no applesauce. I can't take the acidity."

BUT IT WAS Linda who brought the midday meal.

"If I didn't have this work to do," he said, "I could easily go to the dining room and eat with the young and healthy ones."

"Yes, I'm sure you could."

"But I imagine they talk all the time," he said. "I bet they hardly give themselves time to chew for all the talking."

"Yes," said Linda, "there's a helluva lot of talking."

He also suspected that talking had deteriorated during all the years he hadn't been participating in it, that it had emptied of content and dignity and coherence. Present-day conversation would probably just frighten him or confuse him, and he wouldn't be surprised if pure and simple gossip hadn't gone even more downhill than conversation.

As he sat at the table and started eating his lobscouse, she went over and looked at his notebook.

"I like your handwriting," she said. "I especially like

your capital letters. And those little curls at the ends of the words."

"I write the way I learned a hundred years ago," he said. "The letters I use are Mr. Lidén's. He was a schoolteacher who had acquired them in Härnösand when he himself was a boy. They might be any age at all, those letters."

"Your numerals are nice too," she said. "You're already on page 53."

But that was a concept he could not accept: already. Not already, there was no such thing for him as already. You might equally well say that it was pretty poor going that he had only gotten as far as page 53, that he should have completed several hundred pages long ago, that he had been interrupted and delayed, that he was doing everything too far after the event. He often thought to himself not yet, sometimes even still or again, but already or as soon as were not concepts he was prepared to accept.

"Could you pour me a glass of brandy?" he asked. "It's in the drawer under the bed."

She poured him half a glass, saying, "You shouldn't drink."

She sat down on the little blue stool which he kept his clothes on overnight. He had his alarm clock standing on the floor.

"Brandy sobers me up," he said. "It's good to have a clear head. Some time way back I was starting to get a bit muddle-headed, but that won't happen again."

He repeated the expression muddle-headed and chewed on it for a while, exactly as he had chewed on the lobscouse.

"How do you think it's going yourself?" Linda inquired.

"What?"

"This writing."

"That's a question," he said, "that you don't ask a person who writes."

Writing was so hard and so stressful that it couldn't and shouldn't be talked about under any circumstances. There was an enormous gulf between writing and talking. Especially if you were writing out of a sense of duty, because anything else would be gross neglect, verging on a sin of omission. He would like her to know that he often looked back wistfully to the time of not writing and the wild but pleasing emptiness devoid of people. But he was forced to live in a way that was not himself and write something other than what he thought, and think something other than what he expected of himself. He wrote from memory, memory being the only reality there is. No one can write from fleeting enthusiasm or passion, you have to write from self-control and restraint, in a state of immutable constancy. What has been is just as important as what has never been. Nothing is absurd. No, she should never ask how it was going, he didn't know himself, and if he knew he wouldn't be able to put it into words, not even if he were unexpectedly and artfully to say to her, "Why do you never ask how it's going?" Not even then should she ever put the question to him!

"I've mended your tie," she said.

He stopped his little lecture and, still eating his lobscouse, took a sip of brandy and straightened himself up so that she could fasten it under his collar.

"It doesn't look too good," she said. "But it's a strange material, hard and stiff. I've never seen cloth like it."

"That's fine," he said. "The main thing is that it's mended."

Most difficult of all, he went on, was to be simultaneously, quite literally, in every word and every punctuation mark, completely truthful and absolutely untruthful. Veracious mendacity had to be carried through wholeheartedly and with a singleness of purpose comparable to that of a Polar explorer.

BUT MOST TIME-CONSUMING of all is everything that cannot be written, he said. He had finished his meal. He was doing his exercises, a dozen arms-up-and-arms-out, probably to get his digestive processes working.

"What do you mean?" Linda asked.

"I mean everything I have to leave out," he said. "Everything that's not essential."

In fact omitting and abridging took up most of his time, he said. Reality included enormous numbers of events that didn't need to be described in writing, that in many cases could even do harm if they were written. They existed or took place, but were, when you thought about it, superfluous or obvious yes, obvious was the right word. At worst they could break up whole sentences into fragments. Not writing this or that took him as much time as actually writing something.

"And what is it that you avoid writing about?"

"Roads," he said. "And verges and everything that grows on them. Trees and the way they bend and sigh when the wind blows. Flocks of birds. Dogs barking in the distance. The gaps between houses. Exaggerated sensitivity. Clouds and the sun and evening skies and storms in the fall, the weather in general. And people's facial expressions, which are basically indescribable. People just say something or other, and all we can know about them is what they say. And what they say is hardly ever the truth. So, you have to refrain from writing most things."

"And yet," said Linda, "you manage to write so much!"

What people dream in their sleep also had to be left out. Dreams are frail and brittle, they don't lend themselves to written description. And absolutely not to being read. If you're reading a book and come to a dream, you should skip those pages. Dreams could mean anything. Or rather, they meant nothing. It was different with the wakeful dreams of daylight hours, at least if they were written down.

"I'd never thought about that," said Linda. "There's never really been any distinction for me between dreams and everything else."

"I dream complex and detailed dreams at night," he said. "But I never write them down. Mostly I dream about food I'm eating."

"I mostly dream about long journeys," said Linda. "I travel to far-off countries with roses and pelargoniums in bloom by the roadside. And the sun is strong and hot and the clouds as small and insubstantial as snowflakes. And there's a red sky in the evening and the trees are sighing in the breeze and people have cheerful expressions on their faces and there are flocks of birds in the sky chirping and singing the whole time."

He had stood up and was now over at his writing-desk again.

"If you like," he said, "you can borrow the pages I've written and read them. Some time when you've got a moment."

"I'd like to," she said. "Yes, I'd like that."

"I don't write particularly well," he said. "Not like a real writer. I never have. Real writers seem to know everything. But I do my best."

She made a thick roll of the pages he handed her and put it into one of the pockets of her light-blue cotton overall. When she had collected the remains of the meal and took the tray to leave, he told her he used to write a long time ago for an editor who had the imprudence, the impudence even, to say that he wrote too much, too circumstantially and long-windedly!

"Can you imagine!" he said.

10

So when Robert Maser moved into Matilda Holmström's house, Lars Högström the schoolteacher was already installed in what had become known as the teacher's apartment at Eva Marklund's. Robert Maser had it drawn to his attention, as something that possibly could be of interest to him, in Bertil's opinion. One afternoon when Maser was fetching water from the well across the road, Bertil stepped out from a copse and said, "The new schoolteacher is living at Mrs. Marklund's. I just thought you might like to know."

"What's his name?" Robert Maser asked.

"Lars Högström," said Bertil. "He asks questions all the time. He wants to know everything."

"I've got nothing to hide," said Robert Maser.

"You're fetching water for the stew-pot," said Bertil.

"Yes," said Robert Maser. "I'm going to try to make some Swedish hash."

He had bought a pig's head from the widow of Elis in

Lillåberg. In Avabäck he had exchanged one of his ties for a calf knuckle. He had bought onions in the village. He had found the mincer, somewhat rusty, in the house.

"What gives you the right," demanded Bertil, "to try to make hash? You're not from around here."

"It's an experiment," said Robert Maser. "A very modest experiment. I don't imagine for a moment that I'll be able to achieve anything that even approaches Eva Marklund's hash."

> Recipe revealed in a dream. Boil almond potatoes until mushy and stir into leftovers of pea-soup and lightly salted diced pork. Add a few spoonfuls of barley-meal. Form into little cakes or balls and fry in butter. Serve with slices of cooked meat, and lingonberry sauce if desired.

But, he continued, still with the water pail in his hand, he wanted to establish and consolidate the idea of hash in his own mind, Avabäck hash. There was nothing fundamentally wrong with imitations and forgeries if they simply served to convey to us a faint aroma or taste suggestive of the genuine and authentic. How often do we not have to content ourselves with the fragmentary and defective and worthless? He had lived an unsettled and insecure life. He had never had the privilege of any real town to call his own. Now he had found Avabäck. In the evenings the setting sun gave the marshes a tinge of red flecked with gold. This morning he had seen cranes flying south. The almond potatoes he had bought in Vormträsk were a first-class delicacy. He knew, or at least he had been told, that when spring came the cloudberry bushes would be in bloom, the pike would be sporting down at Avaträsk fen, especially in Lomvik creek, the squirrels in the big fir tree between the barns would be building their dray and raising their young, the birch trees would be in gossamer leaf, and the cranes would be back. It was still too soon to say anything definite, but Avabäck could be a potential home. He could even allow himself the whimsical notion that here on the edge of the pine forest, with the extensive Avabäck marsh behind the house and the magnificent willowherbs, though here they were called fireweed, around the woodshed and the outhouse and it was a shame that the flowers were fading now but the hares would come and eat them anyway that this was a place he could pretend or imagine to himself he could call home.

"That's why I'm fetching water for the hash," he said.

"BUT IT'S STILL a mystery to us how you could have ended up here," said Bertil.

The truthful answer to that question would have run something like this:

When the war in Germany was nearing its conclusion, Robert Maser, then going by the name of Martin Bormann, set various plans in motion. He had two passports made for himself, that is to say Robert Maser, one German and one Swedish. He requisitioned a Scania-Vabis bus from the Eastern Front, equipped it with Swedish license plates, painted it white and emblazoned it with big red crosses. He filled the interior with fabrics, not just cloth for sale by the yard but also suits, shirts, dresses, coats, ties and undergarments, all products emanating from the ersatz industry under the ministerial charge of Albert Speer. More specifically, the bus's cargo comprised articles variously manufactured from wood fibers, sugar beet and potato peel, pea-pods, grass, and glue from animal hooves.

At the time of the final or at least provisional defeat of the German Reich, Robert Maser and his bus were in Wahlstorf in Holstein. From there he drove via Plön, Eutin, and Timmendorf to Travemünde. Not once was he stopped, no one asked his business; he bought twenty liters of gasoline from an English patrol and paid with forged pound notes.

When he arrived in Trelleborg on the Salén-Line boat from Lübeck he was welcomed by extremely polite border guards. They even saluted him and the uniform he had selected especially for the occasion.

"You're the last," they told him. "We thought everyone had come by now."

"I was held up," said Robert Maser. "The situation in Germany is terrible."

"We know," said the border guards. "We've seen enough to know how it is."

"It's worse than anyone could ever imagine," said Robert Maser. "There seems to be a direct correlation between human pain and suffering on the one hand, and disorder, traffic chaos, ruins, fire-ravaged forests, empty fields, and starving animals on the other."

"We know. We read the newspapers. We listen to the radio. You can't help being affected by it."

"Personal experience bears no relation to newspaper reports and hearsay and news photographs," he said.

"There's no way to knowledge except through experience. Knowledge and memory are one and the same, there's no knowledge without memory. Here I am stuffed with memories, memories of my frightful journey from Wahlstorf to Travemünde and here you are with what you've heard at second hand."

"Well," said the border guards, "we're Swedes. We're only Swedes."

One of them, peering in through the windows of the bus, said, "You've bandaged them up good and proper. It's hard to believe those bundles are living people, that they'll ever be able to get up again."

"We had to leave everything behind," said Robert Maser. "It's quite an art. When you abandon your memories you abandon all your knowledge too. It's like being reborn. Is that really the sun setting over there?"

"Yes," said the border guards. "We have the best sunsets in Sweden, the most colorful. It's because of the sea and the Kågeröd sandstone."

"Can you gentlemen tell me," Robert Maser inquired, "where I can find a well-stocked paint store?"

"Karl Ask's Paints here in Trelleborg. There's no better paint store in the whole of Sweden."

They even pointed out the way for him. It wouldn't be difficult to find.

"Artists come from far and wide to buy their paints from Karl Ask's," one of the guards remarked. "And some come to stay here to do their painting. Richard Björklund has captured these sky-blue waters with their shifting glints of emerald green beyond the harbor many times. You can almost make out Bornholm or Rügen."

"Whereas Pär Siegård," said one of the others, "mostly turns to the land for his inspiration. Beyond his horizons, north of his horizons, as it were, lies the whole of Sweden."

"Is that your most urgent need right now?" one of them asked, his tone scarcely concealing his amazement and mistrust. "Paint?"

"They've got to have some form of occupation," Robert Maser replied, nodding towards the inside of the bus. "It's hard to get back to normal life. They need implements. In that respect paint and paintbrushes are second to none. What was that artist's name Siegård?"

"That's right, Pär Siegård."

And Robert Maser turned his gaze landwards, as if trying to discern the Siegård horizons beyond the outlines of the houses.

"God bless you!" said the guards as he started the engine prior to moving off.

"Thanks and the same to you," he replied.

He bought two cans of paint at Karl Ask's, light green and black. He found a clump of trees just past Börringe monastery, beside a narrow road leading to Nyhus, where he could carry out his work in peace. He painted the whole bus in green first of all. Then he went to sleep for the night on two of the bales of cloth that he had been using as a bed for some time. By morning the green paint was dry. Then he painted in large lettering along both sides of the bus: MASER'S SUPERIOR QUALITY FABRICS, the name of the company he had, with such foresight, registered with the appropriate Swedish authorities. Beneath these straight horizontal words he added, in an upward arc: ALL THE LATEST FASHIONS.

"FOR INSTANCE, HAVE you soaked the pig's head the way you should?" Bertil continued. "The way it's always been done in these parts?"

"In three lots of water over two days," said Robert Maser.

"And cleaned out the nostrils? And scrubbed around the teeth?"

"Yes," said Robert Maser. "And pricked the eyes."

It was already simmering. The kitchen smelled of bay leaves and cloves. Robert Maser put the calf knuckle into the pot, Bertil helping him to reduce the draft by partially closing the damper. As it grew dark in Avabäck they sat on the kitchen bench that Matilda Holmström had left behind and waited for it to cook thoroughly.

It was nearly midnight when they stood at the sink picking the cooked meat off the bone. It was still hot and blistered their fingers. They put it all through the mincer and back in the stock, brought it to a boil again and then left the incipient hash on the stairs to cool.

But the following day it was still liquid, a gray sludge with the solids sunk to the bottom. Later on Robert Maser stewed some potatoes and carrots in it and ate it as broth.

ON THE NEXT occasion Linda made time to sit with him in his room in Sunnybank Rest Home he said, "But I never dream during the day. You can't dream and write simultaneously."

She had brought back all his completed pages, and, sitting on his bed, had also read the last few pages that he had written since.

"When I was young," he was saying, "we used to dream about everything there might be down south. We dreamt of a direction, you might say. And some of them went off and disappeared in that direction."

"But you stayed," she said.

"I had a touch of TB. You don't travel south with TB."

"And then you started writing for the newspaper?"

But he had nothing to say about writing for the newspaper.

"Sometimes," he said, "I can't help wondering what you all dream about nowadays."

"We dream about mines," she said.

"Of course," he said. "Mines."

"We go around with our hammers and goggles and maps and knives and lamps, and knock chips and chunks off boulders and mountains. You never know."

"Have you tried Avaberg mountain?"

"No," said Linda. "Where is it?"

"It's the huge mountain above Avabäck. There might be just about anything up there."

She tried to persuade him to sit down beside her on the bed. "You really ought to rest," she said. "The working day is over. Hear that? They're ringing in the Sabbath!"

So it was Saturday. The church bells could be heard very clearly.

He stuck his pen down the spiral hinge of his notebook

and sat himself next to her. She took his right hand and laid it in her palm. She inspected the thick, pale blue veins and felt them with her index finger, and gently tapped his long narrow polished nails.

"You've lived for more than a century!"

"It's nothing," he said. "It's nothing."

A hair, one of his new, healthy ones, had dropped down on to his eyelid. She lifted it carefully off between her finger and thumb. Then she kept her hand there, as if she were pointing at his eyes. "You must have seen an incredible amount," she said. "I daren't think about all the things you must have seen."

"No," he said, "it's best not to think about it. If I think about all that I've seen, I start to feel giddy and light-headed. Nobody has the strength to think seriously about what they've seen."

"Sometimes," said Linda, "I sit with old people while they tell me what they think. Actually, old people who think are awful. They ought to have gotten it out of their systems long ago."

Then she added, "But I promise I'll go to Avaberg. For your sake, if nothing else."

Then she asked what was going to happen to Robert Maser next, what he had in mind for that bus, how he would let it find its way to Avabäck, what hindrances and hardships might impede his progress.

"First of all the lettering on the bus has to dry," he replied. "Then Robert Maser will top up the radiator, for which he'll have to go to a nearby farm and fetch water in a tin bucket with a lip. Then when he's driven a few miles he'll make his first sale, an apron with lace trimming around the bib. That'll be to a house near Genarp. He'll be invited in for a meal there too, and with a smile of surprise on his face he'll tuck into a piquant beef stew and have a home-brewed beer with it. Then he'll continue on his way north."

II

"And I shall make him keep to minor roads, he'll have to find his way to the smallest towns and villages. I shall never write that he is shy of people, but I shall make him behave as if he were. He will never park his bus on any square or set up at any market. He is traveling north the whole time. One night near Porrarp a couple of youths break into his bus, not knowing that he is asleep in it, and he beats them off with his measuring rod—he always adds a foot to every order—but he doesn't report them to the local police. He has engine trouble in Ekeberga, and a mechanic from Kosta helps him clean the carburetor. The mechanic is wearing a blue cap with the words Bolinder-Munktell on it in black. 'This engine,' he says, raising his cap to scratch his head, 'has been through a lot.'

"'Does it actually show?' Robert Maser asks. 'The experiences the engine has been through?'

"'The cylinder head has been changed. The distributor is cracked. There are little round holes in the fan and radiator, but they've been plugged. And the ignition leads have been repaired with rubber patches.'

"'But the experiences themselves aren't there to see?'

"'Maybe,' the mechanic from Kosta has to say. 'Maybe to the trained eye.'"

"And Robert Maser commits the expression to memory: the trained eye.

"In Locknevi he sells a woman five yards of sheeting. And I shall have him say, 'This sheeting is just the sort you need, dear lady, it's quite obvious to the trained eye! As far as bed sheets are concerned, you can never be too fastidious!'

"He stays with her the whole winter, and in a few weeks the sheets have worn thin, but that does not seem to bother her. She has lived alone since her fiancé died in Hässelby sanitarium in Mariannelund, and she will take the sheets she inherited from her grandmother out of her linen closet.

"'She wove them from the linen thread she got as maid's wages,' she will say, 'in Vennebjörke before the turn of the century.'

"The house is surrounded by pine forest, the mailbox is on a stake a quarter of an hour away down by the road, the roof of the porch is supported on a round pole.

"'I'm disappointed in these sheets,' Robert Maser will say. 'They haven't lived up to the manufacturer's promises. We've worked them too hard, they were made for a disciplined, lying-still kind of life. Perhaps they were too good for this world and we've misused them. I didn't mean to, I feel quite ashamed of myself.'

"'It doesn't matter,' she will say. 'I never really believed in those sheets.'" But he has to believe, he will say, in his merchandise, he cannot live without faith, what would he be without his fabrics in the bus?

" 'It's rare,' she adds, 'to meet a person who is good through and through.'

"Their conversations will continue more or less all of one winter.

"And when spring comes, I shall let him go on his way, heading northwest. He soon learns to love Swedish place names, they sound so warm and reliable and straightforward in comparison with Mecklenburg names: Bokhyttan, Simonstorp, Granhammar, Västerfärnebo, Ulvshyttan, Gräsmora, Bingsjö, Hemberget, Byvallen, yes, Linda, you can hear him traveling, getting nearer. Now, Linda, you may imagine that his stock might be shrinking in the course of his journey, that he is having trouble supporting himself. But the wood fibers and grass in his cloth do well in the increasingly Arctic climate, they soak up the mist and the damp air, they swell and rise so that the volume he has in Bastuträsk is roughly the same as it was back in Travemünde."

"WHY COULDN'T HE stay there?" said Linda. "With the woman in Locknevi? Then he would never have needed to come to Avabäck."

"You don't know what writing involves," he said. "You're just a simple care assistant. Have you been to investigate Avaberg mountain?"

"Not yet."

"You might think," he said, "that writing is an easy pastime. You see me here at my writing-stand and you think that at least that way he's helping the days to go by. You don't realize that I'm actually straining myself to the limit, that I'm using up my energy as fast as I'm making it. I'm partly moving backwards in time in my own body, and partly I'm subject to time forcing me to write forwards. By the end of the day I can't manage more than my nightly prayer and dropping into bed."

"Well," she said. "In some ways you're quite exceptional."

"Yes," he agreed, "exceptional." Then he asked, "Do you think I could sometimes finish Robert Maser's utterances with an exclamation mark?"

"You should put exclamation marks whenever they're needed!"

"But he wasn't that sort of a man. When I talked to him I couldn't hear a single exclamation mark. He would mutter and mumble. Not a single exclamation mark."

"You've never talked to him!"

"My interview with him in Berlin in 1943 was printed in the newspaper. You can go and look in the files. That was in his time as Martin Bormann. He wanted to develop animal protection in Europe. Every country was to have the same currency. The road network would be improved, as would maternity support. White veal from southern Europe would be prohibited. Meat should be dripping with dark blood. He loved his children. He had seen the Northern Lights twice, from Königsberg. He liked going for strolls in the Tiergarten. He loved his children beyond all reason. Nothing was more important than social equality. One nation, or at most two or three. He sent his greetings to the Land of the Northern Lights."

"But you've never been to Berlin!"

"Just listen, Linda!" he said. "Listen carefully to this sentence: 'The whole of the Tiergarten, whose half-wild beauty stretches all the way from the Brandenburg Gate to the Landwehr Canal and the Zoo beyond it, was bisected by avenues of trees on both sides, exactly as in the drawings of the planner, Lenné; one ran as far as the Zeltenplatz, and was planted with seven types of trees and crossed by broad paths all the way to the Kleiner Stein and Grosser Stern, and by Hofjägeralle which also led to the Grosser Stern and was even more shaded by double rows of trees.'"

"Do you think, Linda, I could have written those words if I'd never been to Berlin?"

"I don't know," she said. "I've never been to Berlin, either."

"Five streets meet at Potsdamer Platz: Bellevue Strasse, Leipziger Strasse, Saarland Strasse, Schönberg Strasse and one I've forgotten."

"But I've seen Avaberg on the map," Linda said. "You can get there from the north through Lillholmträsk and Gammbrinken."

She dug beneath his pillow and found his blue striped flannel nightshirt. She folded it in half and smoothed it out with the palms of her hands. "Shall I help you?" she asked.

"I don't need that sort of help," he said. "And I always say my prayers while I'm still dressed."

"It's hard to know what any person has been through," Linda continued. "And more to the point what they've never been through."

"You've been out and about hunting for gold, Linda," he said, "so you must know what our district looks like."

Yes, she admitted, she did know.

"It's a desert," he said, "which has to be populated. You can't just leave the bogs and the stony soil and the pine heaths and fir forests, all that wilderness, to its fate. Lillåberg and Avabäck and Inreliden and Gammbrinken and Kullmyrliden.

The only thing to do is to write people into it. That's what I've tried to do all my life, write people into the landscape."

"But it's not completely desolate," she said. "And consumption has been cured."

"The consumption that I refer to in my writings," he said, "can never be cured."

When she got up to go he said, "Maybe I'll say my prayers in my nightshirt after all tonight."

As she undid his tie and took off his shirt and pants and underwear he concluded the section about Robert Maser's journey through Sweden:

"He will wake up one cool August morning in Bränntjärnliden, Linda. He will see the sun rise over Pjäsörn and Sikträsket. He will take a ferry over the channel at Arnberg and then drive through Björknäs and Finnäs. In Gissträsk he will sell a coat to a farmer called Vesterlund. In the afternoon he will drive his bus into the yard of a house in Avabäck, which has nothing but women's garments hanging on the line strung between the birch tree and the corner of the house, and he will walk into Eva Marklund's kitchen. And she will give him his very first taste of Swedish hash."

> **Prayer** for the seventeenth Sunday after Trinity. Lord we pray thee that thy Grace may always prevent and follow us, and make us continually to be given to all good works. Almighty and most merciful God, thou who givest us strength in body and soul, help us to stand on our own two feet. Conserve our memories within us. Do not forsake us, grant our thoughts as much freedom as they can bear. Look with mercy on those who rule over us so that in obedience to thy laws they may strive for justice. Destroy all that must be destroyed. Do not let us who are in thrall to thee commit foolish deeds.
> Thou knowest. Amen.

12

THE AVABÄCK SCHOOLCHILDREN were collected by two Volvo buses from their homes in Lillåberg and Inreliden and Ensamheten and the isolated crofts all around there were even individual children in Åmträsk and Granbergsliden. They were divided into three classes according to age: first, fourth and sixth grade. The bus drivers had been issued with protective face masks by the dispensary nurse, which had to be changed every other day.

Lars Högström assembled the children into two lines and led them into the school hall and allocated them desks, the youngest to the left, the oldest to the right. They had to say the Lord's Prayer standing in the aisles between the desks. When they had sat down, all nineteen of them, he said, "I'm your new teacher. My name is Lars Högström. I've already noticed that some of you are coughing and wheezing. A few of you have been holding your breath and made your cheeks red and puffy trying to suppress your hacking coughs. And the hectic flushes on a number of faces haven't escaped my attention, either. But let me say once and for all: you don't need to restrain your coughs or try to smother them, just let whatever is inside you come out. Don't cover your mouth with your arm, don't rub your throat where the tickle seems to be, don't bother holding your breath unnecessarily! I know your last teacher died, but I intend to survive. You can cough all over me as much as you like, you can even cough more often and more loudly than your chest and windpipe seem to demand. I was once a cougher, I know that coughing and breathlessness become central to our lives, even, if you'll allow the expression, our guiding spirit. But we must simply cough with confidence and vitality and so gradually cough ourselves back to health. I have coughed myself healthy. In fact, more than that: I have coughed myself immune."

And he took the chalk and wrote on the blackboard in big white letters the word IMMUNE.

The oldest children, the ones in grade six, had to write the word in their notebooks. Immune = resistant, they wrote.

"It is my hope," he said, "that in the course of time all of you will be able to go out immune into the world."

Then he sat at the little harmonium and played "Ye clouds and darkness/hosts of night/That breed confusion and affright/Begone! o'erhead the dawn shines clear/The light breaks in and Christ is here."

The children sang with surprising musicality. Some voices faded intermittently but others came in stronger, and even coughs and throat-clearings seemed to be in tune.

"Ångermanland," he said, when the children had sat

down, "Ångermanland is the province that binds our country together, that unites the north with the south, the wild with the tame, the flat with the rugged. Without Ångermanland Sweden would not be a united, homogeneous kingdom. Sweden's mightiest river flows through Ångermanland, the Ångerman River. In all my teaching I shall take Ångermanland as our starting point. Even multiplication tables. What are seven eights? Or five times six? Across the whole landscape of Ångermanland mountain ranges stretch down towards the coast, dividing into a myriad of branches, with lakes large and small filling the valleys, narrowing to rivers, every single one of almost indescribable beauty. Five times six is thirty."

WHEN THE FIRST day of term was over, Bertil said, "You really are a proper schoolteacher. You could be the best we've had."

"How can you tell?" asked Lars Högström. "Were you there?"

"I was behind the stove," said Bertil.

"Behind the stove?"

"I see to the heating in the winter," Bertil said. "There's a hatch in the wall where I crawl in."

"So I can never know whether you're present in the classroom or whether you're elsewhere?"

"That's right," said Bertil.

They were sitting in the inner of the two rooms of what was known as the teacher's apartment. Bertil had come creeping up the stairs and entered without knocking. It was after dinner. Eva Marklund had given him herring rissoles with currant sauce. And she had used up the remains of the previous day's veal steak.

"You're watching me," said Lars Högström. "You seem to be keeping me under observation."

"I keep everything under observation," said Bertil.

"I have also been watching you," said Lars Högström. "And not without some curiosity."

"Then you can't be surprised," said Bertil, "if I in turn keep an eye on you."

Lars Högström lit the lamp in the ceiling. It had a flat porcelain shade that spread the light evenly over the room.

"There's something strange," he said, "something quite weird, not to say startling, about your appearance. But I can't put my finger on it."

"No," said Bertil, screwing up his eyes, "it's not all that easy to describe. No one here in Avabäck has worked it out. The midwife spotted it, but no one since. And she's dead now."

"Can it be your eyes?" Lars Högström wondered. "Or your mouth? Or the relationship between your short nose and high forehead?"

Bertil was looking at him with an almost imperceptible smile, his cheeks giving the merest hint of a momentary twitch. After a while he pulled up the sleeves of his jacket and shirt and held out his hands with the palms downward.

"Can you see?"

Lars Högström scrutinized the hands. It took him some

time to ascertain what it was that was so remarkable about them.

"They're identical," he said at last. "The warts on your index fingers are exactly the same. The veins are in exactly the same pattern beneath the skin. The creases in the knuckles are the same on both hands."

"Precisely," said Bertil.

"They're the same hands," said Lars Högström, "just a mirror image."

So Bertil took off his shoes and socks and displayed his feet. They too were alike in every detail. There were birthmarks above the two big toes that resembled pine cones.

Concentrating again on his face, Lars Högström could see it straight away: the two halves were exactly alike, the little bags under the eyes, the corners of the mouth, the cheekbones, the pale freckles, even the disfiguring hairs on his cheeks.

"No need to show me any more," he said, as Bertil started unbuckling his belt to remove his pants.

"You can see it?"

"Yes," Lars Högström said. "I can see it."

"Other people are composed of quite dissimilar halves," said Bertil. "Two halves that often contradict and oppose each other, that in fact are incompatible. Half of a face may hate the world, the other half be filled with love and concern. The normal person lacks consistency and unity. There are two conflicting souls in the breast of the ordinary person. But my scrotum hangs absolutely straight and my balls are both the same size."

"I believe you," said Lars Högström.

"For instance, if you look at Eva Marklund downstairs," said Bertil, "who gave you herring rissoles today, you can see right away how split and unevenly balanced she is. And she's not as bad as some."

"That's true," said Lars Högström.

"As far as I know," said Bertil, "there aren't any other equilateral people. No one else who is his own mirror-image. His own twin, as the midwife once said. Her name was Morin and she was born in Kvarnberg. She got cancer. I just happened to be perfect. It wasn't that I deserved it. It just happened that way."

"I understand," said Lars Högström.

"What is incomprehensible," he continued, "is that I didn't see it before. Now that you've pointed it out to me, all I can see is just how symmetrical you are."

"You probably realize," said Bertil, "that those of us who've been created this way have certain obligations. If we don't have the duality that everyone else suffers from, it's our duty to keep our eyes open."

"Of course," said Lars Högström.

"I hope and assume you won't say anything," Bertil added. "That you won't betray the confidence I've entrusted to you."

"I would never betray a confidence," Lars Högström reassured him. "No one can entice or cajole me into anything. I'm insusceptible."

They sat in silence for a long time, each immersed in his own, completely separate, thoughts. The bulb under the flat porcelain shade shone down upon them.

Finally Bertil said, "I often think about you and Eva Marklund alone in this house. And that there's only a staircase between you. And that you each sleep in your own bed."

"I'd never thought about it," said Lars Högström.

"If you do start to think about it, you ought to be aware that you can't do anything without being noticed. No person can ever be really alone."

"Nor is that," said Lars Högström, "anything I'd ever thought about."

13

LINDA OFTEN USED to come to his room after everyone had had their dinner and sleep had descended on Sunnybank Rest Home.

This time she was carrying a small rucksack full of gravel and splinters of rock.

"I've never understood it," he said. "There were mines in Adak and Kristineberg and Boliden and Renström, where they dug up silver and gold and tin and nickel, but I never understood it. During the war they filled up vehicles with producer gas in Avabäck."

"You've got to have an eye for it," she said. "For things that just look like rock, but are really the greatest secrets that lie buried in the earth."

And she pulled out a selection from her limp rucksack to show him: arsenopyrite, calcite, copper pyrite, pegmatite, zinc blende and magnetite.

"If you've found all this," he said, "I don't understand

why you're here as a care assistant. You should be queen of a mining empire."

"It's not good enough," she said. "The mineral content is too low. And the ore seams are too small."

But he had to admit that many of the chunks and shards and fragments that she was showing him glistened and gleamed like precious stones, or like ice crystals on the windowpane in winter.

"We're all searching," she said. "You never know."

"The era of minerals is past," he said. "Who's bothered about metals nowadays? The time of solid substances is more or less over. You ought to be looking for gases and vapors and fantasies. While you're young."

"You'll never be a mineral prospector?" she asked.

"No, never."

"This," she said, holding up a lump of stone, "is granite."

He conceded that he recognized that: his own yard had been full of it.

"But the only thing that lasts," he said, "is the transient and impermanent."

Then he asked, "And Avaberg?"

No, she had still not made it to Avaberg.

She went on to mention that a couple of people would like to come and visit him. The minister was hoping for a spiritual chat. And a professor from Umeå, a gerontologist, wanted to see him and possibly also examine him. Or at any rate just look in.

"By all means," he said. "Let them come! I've got all the time in the world."

BEFORE SHE LEFT she stood and read the last few pages he had written:

That was how duet singing came to Avabäck. Lars Högström the schoolteacher happened to pass Matilda Holmström's house on his evening walk. The sound of Robert Maser's strong voice was audible outside, a clear tenor that hardly seemed to belong in deepest Västerbotten. "Joy," he was singing, "is like a wench who's loath to stay, Her favors don't last long. From your weary brow she smoothes the cares away. A kiss and then is gone."

A few days later Robert Maser happened to be strolling past the Marklund house just as Lars Högström was practicing Fröding's "Helicon's Flower," set to music by Ture Rangström. Robert Maser could even see him: he was standing in front of the hall mirror studying the movements of his mouth and throat as he sang. His voice was a somewhat muffled but sonorous baritone, resonating through the thin, sawdust-insulated walls of the Marklund house.

And for the next couple of weeks they both continued their two-mile walks to hear whether the other one might be singing again. And they were. Or rather, each sang alone while the other stood outside in the damp evening darkness, leaning against a birch

> The composer **Ture Rangström** has died at the age of 63. He leaves four symphonies, a number of symphonic poems, and a rich legacy of settings for verse. He acquired his musical education in Germany, mainly under Pfitzner, but spent his whole productive lifetime in Stockholm and devoted himself particularly to Swedish poetry.
>
> Rangström was the one outstanding genius among contemporary native composers.
>
> His final resting-place is in Gryt churchyard, Östergötland.

trunk, listening discreetly. They sang for each other without being aware of it, or at least, pretending not to know.

During Lars Högström's singing practice Eva Marklund used to open the kitchen door so that the exquisite sounds from the teacher's apartment above would filter down and into her rooms.

One afternoon, as the children were leaving the classroom, Bertil emerged from behind the stove and said, "I think you ought to go in to Matilda Holmström's house and introduce yourself, not just stand behind a tree trunk listening in secret."

In fact, he would venture to suggest that this clandestine and deceitful lurking in the darkness seemed almost perverse or warped and was not the sort of thing people did in Avabäck. A real inhabitant of Avabäck would stride through the door and come straight out with it, without any prevarication, would say how captivated and enchanted he was by the singing he had overheard, that he shared this passion for music and song completely and whole-heartedly, that he would be delighted to take part in any music practice, and that he was himself a reasonable baritone and could sight read.

For the inhabitants of Avabäck, said Bertil, openness and honesty were what was valued most, particularly in strangers.

Three male voices would be no bad thing, said Lars Högström. Could Bertil not consider lending his hand to the pump? A trio would open up a myriad of possibilities. It really didn't need to be a trained voice or a big one.

But Bertil shook his head.

A voice is always a voice, Lars Högström continued to urge him. Three-part harmony is particularly suited to hymns, Negro spirituals, and folk-songs.

No, Bertil could not. It was one of the disadvantages of symmetricality that he could not distinguish one note from another or one harmony from another. He might just about understand rhythm, but not notes or harmonies. Music was actually an expression of the tensions and contradictions in human beings themselves. The musical person could recognize in notes and harmonies the conflicts in his own breast.

SO LARS HÖGSTRÖM knocked on Robert Maser's door, opened it and went in. He hadn't come for anything special, not at all, he just happened to be passing and wanted to say hello, no more than that. Up here in the wilds where people were few and far between everyone ought to know of each other's existence.

"My name is Lars Högström," he said. "I'm a teacher."

And Robert Maser explained that he was a clothier. At present. The future might bring something different. Crockery and glassware. Or food.

"Have you, Mr. Maser, had the chance to sample the local hash?" Lars Högström asked.

Yes, he had. And he would never forget it. It had certainly given him something to think about.

He was sitting on the kitchen bench, leaning forward with his hands on his knees. Lars Högström was still standing a couple of feet inside the door. The kitchen stove was lit, the damp wood sizzling as it burned.

"Can I offer you a drop of water?" Robert Maser asked.

"That would go down a treat!" said Lars Högström.

So Robert Maser filled the metal scoop in the water

bucket and handed it to him. Lars Högström drank a few sips and said, "Exceptionally good water. Water is unsurpassed as a food. Even if it sometimes has a slight flavor of rust or moss. Best water I've tasted!"

Then he emptied the scoop in a single gulp and replaced it in the bucket.

As the scoop knocked against the cracked enamel it emitted a strangely vibrating tone, like the sound of a distant church bell. And Lars Högström remarked that the scoop and the bucket and the water together produced a sound that was musically rather fascinating.

"You're interested in music, then?" said Robert Maser. "Won't you sit down?"

And Lars Högström sat down on the rickety spindle-back chair between the kitchen bench and the sink.

"I often sing when I'm alone," Robert Maser went on. "Folk songs or ballads or some aria or other."

"I sing when I'm on my own too," said Lars Högström.

"I think I also play the piano," said Robert Maser.

"You think you do?"

"I'm suffering from loss of memory," said Robert Maser. "I know practically nothing about myself. But I'm evidently a musical person."

And he attempted to elucidate:

He had suddenly woken up as a traveling clothier here in Sweden. He had no idea where he came from. The only thing he remembered was Mecklenburg, but even that was very hazy: large pigsties, huge fields of corn, sugar beet and potatoes. He wanted to live a simple and uncomplicated life here in Avabäck, without connections, present or past. When he said he was suffering from memory loss, that was not entirely correct. He was not suffering. He felt no need for memories. He had bought some sheet music of songs by Ture Rangström and August Söderman in Skellefteå, and they had given him great pleasure, in particular "I see the stars fill the skies with their twinkling glow."

Could he perhaps, he concluded, be of service with a shirt? Or a tie? Or maybe even a suit and waistcoat?

No, Lars Högström had all the clothes he needed. He only wore shirt and pants when he was teaching. But it had struck him, as he listened to Robert Maser's account, that there was an element of memory loss in his own life too. A kind of physical memory loss. He had been seriously and chronically sick, but had recovered. And his return to health had been so radical and definitive that his body no longer knew what sickness was, it had become immune, and he was suffering from what might be described as a lack of anxiety, despair or despondency, which was closely akin to memory loss.

Robert Maser said he dimly recognized the phenomenon, and if he had still possessed his memory he would probably have been able to describe similar cases. His ties, he should add, were mainly black and red patterned.

WHAT LARS HÖGSTRÖM missed most here in Avabäck, he said quietly, almost to himself, was the ensemble, or collective, music-making that had formed an important part of his life for some years: singing in a choir or quartet or trio. Otherwise there was virtually everything he needed in Avabäck, but singing, in unison or in parts, was hard to be without.

"Duets can provide considerable satisfaction," said Robert Maser. "Duets should never be underestimated."

Lars Högström opened his trench coat and drew out two music quartos from his inside pocket.

"As chance would have it, Mr. Maser," he said, "I have here a selection of songs for two male voices. Just happened to have them on me, as they say."

And he handed Wennerberg's *Student Songs* to Robert Maser, who immediately started leafing through them, reading and humming to himself.

Pulling off his coat, Lars Högström made his way to the kitchen bench.

And soon they were singing, at first a trifle hesitantly and restrained, but then at full pitch and with deep feeling: "The world does yet no corner hold/Where a man can act both big and bold/Go at it like an infidel/And yet avoid the path to hell" and "My soul and mind do trouble me/The outcome is not clear to see."

When they finally took a break to get their breath back, the flow of their conversation was quite different from what it had been before the singing.

"You've got a much lighter voice than I imagined," said one.

"Your gentle vibrato is made for duets," replied the other.

"And you've got an amazing intensity in your dark vowels!"

"But your tone is more natural and open than mine."

They continued singing for a couple of hours, progressing from the *Student Songs* to several psalms and a couple of anthems. Robert Maser showed himself adept at improvising the lower harmony with astonishing skill. Even some of Peterson-Berger's songs were familiar to both schoolteacher and clothier, including "Longing Is My Inheritance" and "A Sound Like Little Violins."

When they finally called it a day they were both rather sweaty, with sore throats and aching jaws. They immediately set a time and place for their next practice.

BERTIL WAS STANDING in the road in front of the house.

"I had no idea," he said as Lars Högström came out, "that people could sing like that! Even on the radio I've never heard anything so powerful and moving!"

"Have you been out here all evening?" Lars Högström asked.

"No," said Bertil. "I took a turn around the house from time to time. And the bus was unlocked. I was okay."

As they walked through the darkness towards the school and the Marklund house Bertil tried humming from memory some of the tunes he had heard. But he really was totally unmusical.

WHEN LINDA HAD finished reading all the new pages he had written, she gathered up her collection of rocks and minerals that were lying around him on the bed. "You write so slowly," she said, "you'll never get to the end."

"I'm not bothered about the end."

"You won't forget the gerontologist and the minister?" she reminded him.

"I haven't even thought about them, so I can hardly forget them."

"And you shouldn't write about Bertil. He's still alive."

"You won't be able to find your way up Avaberg mountain by following the stream," he had just remembered and had to tell her. "It's only visible here and there."

14

A FEW DAYS later, just as he had completed a sentence with the phrase "the refinement of both meat ingredients and taste sensations," the gerontologist arrived. They exchanged greetings and a few words about the time of year: it was misty outside with a touch of frost on the trees and grass, a season that brought cold and darkness not only to nature but also to the human soul.

He put down his pen at once and started to unbutton his shirt to present his chest for examination. But the gerontologist stopped him. No, there was no question of a medical check-up, he didn't even have a stethoscope or any other instruments with him, his business was not of that kind, he wasn't even sure whether he had any business there at all.

"You're writing," he said, nodding towards the writing-stand and notepad.

"Yes. I'm trying to finish a report I began when I was in my prime."

"You've been a writer all your life?"

"I used to write news articles, but I was prevented from doing so for some decades. But apart from that it's what I've always done."

"Do you enjoy it?"

"I don't know whether that's the right word. Enjoy. No, not enjoy. But I construct sentences. And you never know."

"You never know what?"

"I can't really say."

THE GERONTOLOGIST HAD gone over to the window, letting his gaze wander idly over the frozen white landscape. He had a bald pate, with thinning gray hair at the back, and his jacket was crumpled and threadbare. He kept his hands in the pockets of his pants to support his weak, stooped back.

No, when he thought about it, he could only reiterate that he had no real business here. For him it was an excursion, one might almost say excuse, both words could apply. He needed to escape from the hospital in Umeå. He would invent a reason and absent himself, a pretext for the sake of the travel expenses.

"So I am your pretext?"

Well, that was one way of looking at it, and indeed a unique and indisputable pretext from the point of view of both research and expenses. Even if in actual fact it wasn't strictly scientific research. No, it was just absolutely essential for him to get away from Norrland University hospital in Umeå, away from the musty air and human decay. He already knew everything about ageing, everything that was worth knowing, and he didn't want to know any more.

The writer had sat down on the bed, had buttoned up his shirt again, and was leaning back against the wall. A smell of fried fish came wafting along the corridor.

Yes, life as a gerontologist was fundamentally intolerable, and he could only regret his unhappy choice of career. His parents had felt old age approaching and had wanted him to pursue research into it and do something about it. He had been forced to take on the horrors of ageing and incorporate them into his own life. For many years now he had been dependent on medicines for his chronic bouts of depression, which were entirely rational and based on his knowledge. His field of research, old age, was a subject that decency demanded should be left in peace. Old age should be shrouded in mystery rather than investigated. How often had he not cursed the politicians and officials who had decided that gerontology was a valid field for research? He wished them dead on an almost daily basis! There was no other publicly-funded activity that involved such an outrageous and literal squandering of taxes! Everything was actually so simple: the heart's capacity to pump blood fell by half, the speed of nerve impulses dropped by a third, the kidneys and lungs lost much of their efficiency, the brain shrank. Anyone who had ever studied an old person's withered brain cells under a microscope never forgot it, or only forgot it in old age. Their dry, wrinkled skin could provide no long-term abode for any soul or spirit.

Sitting on the bed, the writer occasionally raised his right hand in a gesture of agreement to show that he was listening and understood. He even attempted to insert a couple of passing contributions into the professor's monologue: he too had once aged, he was no stranger to decline and failing strength and humiliation, and deep down he was a little ashamed of his positive outlook on life, his optimism and his fortitude, for which of course there was no rational basis.

But the hardest thing, said the academic from Umeå, addressing himself to the window and the sterile landscape, was the realization that nothing, absolutely nothing, could be regarded as constant or reliable. Everything, everything in the whole of Creation, was twisted and contorted and even turned into its opposite by the inexorable march of time. It had probably been forever thus. Decent people were transformed into monsters. Mass murderers lost their memories and became as pious as choirboys; during a service they could sing wholeheartedly, "O Lord, deal not with us after our sins, neither reward us after our iniquities." And the supporters and inciters of mass murderers would suddenly start preaching the gospel of love and the skin of wolves would sprout the soft wool of sacrificial lambs. The soul of man was a product of the imagination, erratic and impulsive, an illusion in the hands of a capricious conjurer. And all this emanated from ageing, that loathsome phenomenon, the movement of the hands on the clock, the changing seasons, the relationship between fertilization and decomposition, the inadequate strength of the cell walls, the insufficient durability of the heart in short, the whole repugnant field that constituted gerontology.

"But what if everything inverts itself? If someone survives old age and begins to live in reverse, so to speak?"

"I know, I know! But what's the point of it? That too ends in extinction, though from the other direction."

"So is there no solace for us?"

That was the question one encountered so often in the care of the elderly and geriatric research. In fact it was probably that very quest for consolation that provided the rationale for the whole enterprise. And perhaps many old people found comfort in natural ways, so to speak: in absent-mindedness and confusion, declining faculties, and in some cases through an almost perverse concentration on physical infirmities and deformities like fractured hips, fungal infections of the mouth, nervous tremors, or phantom aches in amputated limbs. Total disintegration then became a distant blurred horizon, far beyond the pain and distress of the moment. But for him, the gerontologist, who was forced to participate in the damnation of old age while still in his own prime of life, there was no escape or consolation. He had tried cannabis and tobacco, but neither helped. He had loved his wife, to no avail. In music and poetry and theater he had found only deeper despair. He had traveled abroad many times, but not even the most famous and magnificent tourist attractions or sights had offered him any solace, they seemed only to crumble and collapse before his very eyes. And he did not understand religion, he was simply impervious to it. He liked to quote a wise German on the subject of old age: "A bitter drop of poison that renders the whole of life repulsive!" It was in old age that the meaninglessness of life manifested itself, it was the ultimate proof of the absolute power of nature and gravity.

"Gravity?"

"Yes, gravity."

"I've got a bottle of brandy under the bed. But I can see it would be wasted."

"Yes. It would be wasted."

"When I was even younger and living in Avabäck," said the writer, "there were lots of people who died in the prime of life. They never got old, consumption took them."

But even tuberculosis was in essence a sort of ageing, according to the latest research. The mycobacteria go into a temporary frenzy and attack organs and tissues and cells, and the organs and tissues and cells defend themselves by racing through their entire life-cycles in the shortest possible time, the parts of the body under attack resist and break into a gallop, blood vessels burst and the lung alveoli collapse; in short, the whole body, the whole individual, matures and declines and ages in a manner that can only be described as hectic or feverish or exaggerated. But there is no doubt that it is an ageing process.

"I'd never thought of that."

"The world is full of things that no one but a gerontologist would ever have thought of."

"It's hard," said the man sitting on the bed, "just observing and registering and noting without being directly involved."

"Yes," said the man at the window, "it is."

"But this is not an examination?"

"No," said the gerontologist, "this is not an examination at all."

And he added that he had promised himself never to carry out any more examinations in his life.

"Won't you even read through what I've just written, on the writing-stand over there?"

Well, he could do that. Written words and pages didn't need to be examined, notes could just be glanced through and that was the end of it. It was more or less like looking out at the landscape through a train window.

He was a fast reader. He went over to the writing-stand, took out his reading glasses and put them on. When he no longer had his hands in his pockets his back became even more bent and stooped.

"Yes," he said when he had finished reading, "you certainly can write. I wish it had come as easily to me when I was writing my dissertations and reports."

"If you stay for a bit," said the man who had written what had just been read, "I'm sure you can have some of the lunch that's on its way. We'll probably find things to talk about."

But the professor from Umeå declined, he had long ago had enough of the fried fish and creamed spinach and overcooked potatoes of rest homes.

"But if it had been hash . . ." he said.

The hash from around here was well known and highly thought of even among academics in Umeå.

"We only get that once a fortnight. And it's so insipid, as if diluted. There's no goodness in municipal hash."

These were the pages the gerontologist had read so speedily at the writing-stand, perhaps all too speedily and as if already on the point of departure:

IT WAS ABOUT then that Manfred Marklund came home on a short visit to Avabäck, on leave from the hospital. His right lung had been treated with gas, which meant that he was not infectious for the time being and the hospital doctors had granted him a few days' break.

> **Gas treatment**. Localized treatment for tuberculosis of the lungs, also called collapse therapy. Air or nitrogen is introduced into the pleura to cause the lung to collapse so that it no longer functions in the breathing process. The collapsed lung will sometimes heal of its own accord.

Eva was standing on the steps waiting for him. She had heard the taxi.

"I hardly recognized you," she said.

"But you look the same," he responded.

"You've gotten so thin. And I've never seen that suit before."

"There's a royal fund," he said. "They buy shirts and suits for us. And ties. The Oscar II Fund."

Once inside in the lobby she took his hands and examined them. The calluses were gone, his nails were trimmed and clean, his fingers lay white and delicate in the palms of her hands.

And the wart above the thumbnail had gone.

"What have they done with your hands?" she asked.

"They look like a schoolteacher's hands. The skin is really translucent, you can see right into the veins. And the scar from the plane doesn't show any more. And your wedding ring looks as if it might slip off at any moment."

He smiled at her in polite agreement. Yes, he admitted, he had changed, he was no longer the same person. He was aware of it himself. He had not realized before that he was changeable.

"I always thought you were as you were meant to be," she said.

"But you're as attractive as ever," he said. "If you had more chance to rest and weren't weighed down with responsibility for everything, you'd be a beauty."

"Fancy seeing you in glasses!" she said.

"They're reading glasses," Manfred Marklund replied. "They're for reading."

"And your cheeks," she said. "They're as smooth as the inside of my thighs."

"I shave with a razor," he said. "In the mornings. I get a new razor blade every week. And they've given me a bottle of after-shave lotion."

"But you've gotten furrows in your brow that you didn't have before."

"The creases in my brow have come because I think about things now that I never thought about before. Thinking in Avabäck was like running on glassy ice. When I've done with reading for the day, I go over to the mirror to see how the creases have grown."

"You never used to read before."

"I used to read the paper. The Phantom hunting down the villains. President Truman facing re-election by a narrow margin. Johan Anton Åström from Morön dead."

"I didn't know you were so inclined," she said.

No, he hadn't known it himself.

He sat down at the kitchen table straight away. She already had the enamel pot and the saucepan on the stove, and now she opened the flue to increase the heat.

"The man singing upstairs in the bedroom," she said, "is the new schoolteacher."

"Oh."

"There's a stranger who's moved into Matilda Holmström's house."

"Oh."

"He's a sort of traveling salesman in fabrics and clothes and elastic."

"Oh, I see."

Bertil had come in at the door, sat down on the stool beneath the coat hooks for a while and studied this new and strange Manfred Marklund, then crept out again.

"So what is it that you read?" Eva asked. "All day long."

"There's a library in the sanitarium," he said. "By the time I'm well again, I'll have read every book there. I've got something to aim for. It's a room with nothing else in it but books."

"Any particular books," she wanted to know. What had he been reading most recently, for example?

He didn't need to search his memory. His reading had included such things as:

For more than a hundred thousand years man was an animal that lived in constant fear and thought he would die every time anything sudden or unexpected occurred. He would start to shake and go into a kind of cramp from fear and anxiety. It was the same in the society man now lived in. All his security was based on the unexpected not happening. Society should not be as cruel as life itself. But if the unanticipated or unforeseen happened anyway, and if the person affected didn't face the immediate prospect of death, then he would enter a state of exhilaration, and his soul, having initially shrunk back in fear and cramp, would fly up and unfurl itself and the person would laugh. That was something he had read lately. That abrupt leap from terror to elation and arrogance, that was the comic side of life. But sometimes the exact opposite would occur, and a person would be cast down from recklessness and exhilaration to despair. That is the tragic side of life.

"Well," said Eva, "that sounds like interesting reading."

And she asked whether he still liked as much onion as before.

"Yes, lots of onion."

Something else he had read the other day:

If you have discovered your rational faculties, then you will always feel like a traveler, even if you're not heading for a specific destination, because there isn't any destination. But you get used to keeping your eyes open for everything that takes place in the world. You don't set your heart on anything in particular, you carry your traveling within you and rejoice at reversals and transience. The nights can sometimes be tough, like being in the desert. And some days, he had also read, can be equally miserable, when you encounter nothing but deception and dirt and insecurity. But mostly mornings bring comfort and light, you can rest for a while beneath a leafy tree and take pleasure in the sun. Rationality makes you a morning person, as it were.

"But you don't want me to fry the onions?"

"No. Onions should be left as they are."

"I've added a bit more salt for you."

"Good. Generally people never put enough salt in."

When the meal was ready and she had placed the casserole and dish of almond potatoes on the table, she went out into the lobby and banged on the wall at the foot of the stairs. Lars Högström the schoolteacher came down immediately and they started eating.

"I've had gas treatment," said Manfred Marklund. "So I'm not infectious."

"It doesn't matter," said Lars Högström. "I'm immune. I've been in a sanitarium too. That was where I came to appreciate music, though I wasn't aware of it at the time. They had a gramophone."

"I read," said Manfred Marklund. "There's a lot to read in Hällnäs."

Even when warmed up the hash was dense and firm, the thin rings of raw onion gleaming yellowy-white in the gray mass of minced meat.

"You can't get this kind of baby onion in southern Sweden," said Lars Högström.

"No. There's a lot you can't get in southern Sweden."

Using their forks they mashed up the potatoes with the hash, and Manfred Marklund also let a small lump of butter melt on his plate. They ate with their forks, using the edge of their flatbread to divide just the right-sized morsels of the hash.

Then Manfred admitted frankly why he was there:

He had come home simply for the sake of the hash. It was Eva's hash that was the real object of this leave of absence. It had been on his mind day and night. He could never get anything like it in Hällnäs, and he just had to taste it one more time. Not even the best, most thought-provoking books in the world could compare with Eva's hash.

"When you've regained your health," said Lars Högström, "nothing will ever come between you and hash again."

"If you like," said Eva, "I could try and send you some. I don't see why I shouldn't be able to put some in the mail."

No, that wouldn't be the same. And you could never tell what might happen to things in the mail.

When you were sick but not infectious, life couldn't be better. Although of course he would like to be healthy, in fact he was looking forward to the day when he would be completely well again. Even though he didn't rightly know what he would do when he was back to good health. He didn't want to fritter away his health lumbering or digging ditches. Even as a healthy person he would probably want to carry on living as a sick one.

After they were alone again, when the schoolteacher had returned to his room upstairs to correct schoolwork and sing his scales, and Manfred had scraped the casserole clean with a teaspoon, he said he understood completely, that he realized how things were, that from the very first intimate affectionate tone of her banging on the wainscoting at the foot of the stairs he had seen what was what. He would sleep on the kitchen bench. He didn't mind, he had slept there all through his childhood, he really didn't mind going back to the kitchen bench. He had a book in his coat pocket. He would read his book and then go to sleep. It was only this one night, after all, his night's leave, you might say.

"But there are women in the sanitarium, too, you know," he pointed out. "And not all of them are dying."

15

WHAT WAS IT that Manfred Marklund had understood?

It can hardly have been all this, not all of it:

Late one evening a few weeks before, Eva Marklund had knocked on the wainscoting at the foot of the stairs, a diffident, restrained knocking. Lars Högström had already undressed for the night, always sleeping naked since he knew no sickness could afflict him, so he wrapped himself in his blue terrycloth robe that he had bought from Robert Maser and went down to see what she wanted.

"I forgot the dessert," she said. "I forgot I had a dessert today."

They had had stewed liver with rice that evening. Rice was no longer rationed.

She was sitting on the wood-box, her face unusually pale and her hands tucked into her armpits.

The dessert was in a little dish on the kitchen table in his usual place.

Bertil had brought the dessert, some time before the news on the radio. The war was still going on in Jerusalem. The clothier in Matilda Holmström's house had been to Lycksele, and had gotten the dessert in exchange for something and then passed it on to Bertil. But Bertil hadn't wanted it, thinking it more suitable for a schoolteacher.

It was a slice of almond cake, to which Eva had added a spoonful of raspberry conserve and some whipped cream.

She waited until he had started cutting the cake with his spoon and putting the first pieces in his mouth and then she said, "I can't sleep at night."

"You can't?" he said, as he chewed.

"Sometimes I have such a panic attack that I have to go out on the stairs to breathe."

"Your Manfred will be fine," he said, masticating the almond cake slowly between his teeth. "Science is making huge advances. You don't have to worry."

"It's not Manfred I'm worried about," she said. "I've never been so close to him that I would really miss him. I'm afraid for my own life. Even just being here in Avabäck can be the most delightful life. Even that. I don't want to lose it."

"If you've kept going so far," Lars Högström said with the spoon between his lips, "you'll get over it."

"I can't make myself believe I will," she said, still with her hands tucked under her arms against her ribs. "If only I could believe it."

"Life," he said, "is more or less equally delightful wherever you live it."

"The cloudberries," she said, "on Klappmyrliden hill when

they're ripe. And whitefish roe in the fall. And the newspaper now that nothing happens in Avabäck any more. And the morning sun through the mist in the fall."

"This," he said, "is an almond cake like the ones they make down south, with cream cheese in it."

She couldn't help it, she said, that even when she made an effort to think of sea birds or potato blossom her thoughts always came back to consumption. She thought about it all the time. There was nothing in her house or her surroundings that was not contagious. As soon as she gave the slightest cough the thought sprang into her head that she was infected. She didn't even dare clear her throat. She would never forget Manfred coughing and clearing his throat. The tiniest tickle in any part of her body would immediately fill her with fear. And she was always feeling tickles in her arms and chest and midriff, everywhere in fact. She dared not name all the places in her body where she felt tickling.

"I understand your concern," he said, wiping the cream from the corners of his mouth. "You're the slim, delicate-throated type who is particularly susceptible."

But that had nothing to do with it, Eva opined. She had had a sister called Mildred who was hugely obese. But it hadn't helped her. It was ten years ago this year that she had died of tuberculosis. No, what it came down to was contagion. If you had any contagion near you, you could never be sure. She was probably already ill, maybe even dying, and whatever she did would be too late, and anyway there wasn't anything you could do. Did the almond cake taste the way it should?

"It was excellent. And nothing can touch your whipped cream."

Yes, it was the clothier who had brought it from Lycksele. Bertil had also said it was crazy for such a great guy to live so out-of-the-way as over at Matilda Holmström's, especially as far as singing duets was concerned. Something ought to be done about it.

"Well," said Lars Högström, "your Bertil seems to think of everything and everyone."

"That house is contaminated too," said Eva Marklund. "So many have died there, in the kitchen as well as the bedroom, that I've lost count. The gaps in the floorboards and the joins in the wallpaper are chock-full of contagion. Just like in this house. And the bedsteads."

"When I was in the sanitarium," he said, "we had desserts every single day, and I ate too many of them. But my appetite for them is reviving."

He had stood up and gone over to the window facing the road. There was nothing out there but darkness. He had his thumbs tucked behind the cord of his robe.

"It'll soon be nighttime," Eva Marklund said, "so I'd better try and get some sleep in this wretched bedroom of mine."

Then she added, "You're all right, you've got your immunity."

"It had occurred to me," he said, "it's struck me from time to time, that I might be able to let you share my immunity. At least it might be worth a try."

Eva had also stood up, and was over by the bedroom door.

Yes, she said, the same thought had occurred to her.

"Exactly the same way you inject vaccine into the human body so that it makes itself immune."

Yes, she said, that was just what she had been thinking herself in her desperation.

"It can't do any harm to give it a try."

So he took off his robe, folded it up carefully and laid it on the chair he had sat on to eat his dessert. Then they went into the bedroom together and gave it a try.

AFTER HAVING READ this latest part of his report, Linda finally decided she should go to see the Leader of the District Council.

"Aren't you one of Melker's daughters?" the Councilor asked. "The guy who was on the Council?"

"Yes," Linda replied. "I'm a care assistant at Sunnybank Rest Home."

Then she stated her business:

> **Council Leader.** Elected leader of a local council, appointed by the council. The leader is a political party member. Normally chair of the executive committee. Salaries and other benefits are determined by the council. The leader of the council has full powers over matters concerning local residents.
>
> There are at present approximately 600 local council leaders in the country.

There was this incredibly old man at Sunnybank, a senior citizen well known to everyone in the area. The fact was that he wrote all the time, never stopping, he would stand at his writing-desk day after day. He had been using Council pens and pencils for a long time now, having used up all his own. Even his notebooks were Council ones, and they cost nineteen crowns apiece. He spent his pocket money on brandy.

She had tried to persuade him to take up some other hobby but hadn't succeeded. He didn't want to make knotted rugs in the occupational therapy room downstairs. Nor did accordion playing or devotions in the day-room appeal to him. She felt she had to let the Council know. Because it was in a municipal institution that this unimpeded writing activity was being conducted.

"But what is it he's writing?"

"A newspaper report. An article without beginning or end. Especially without end."

Had she read what he'd written?

Yes she had read the whole of it, as far as she could tell, if it was possible to call it a whole.

And?

So she recounted everything she could remember. She named people by their actual names and told him of their deeds and what had befallen them and where they lived; she may have even added here and there some little detail that might have been lacking in the original, and she also repeated the dialogue she had read and the expressions on people's faces that she had imagined.

The Councilor interrupted her a few times. "Well, well, I'd heard about that," he said. Or, "Well, I'm darned!" Or, "Ah, that's how they've always been in that family!"

"So how much does he write?" he asked.

"At least a page a day," said Linda.

When she got to the end, the very provisional end, he said, "I'm glad you told me all this. You're one of Melker's daughters, for sure. You did right to come to me."

"I thought it was my duty, unfortunately," said Linda.

This was how she concluded her account:

When Lars Högström the schoolteacher lay with Eva Marklund that first time and they had done what they had to do, she sat up in bed, tilted her head towards the ceiling and burst out laughing. She just shot up and stretched back and simply roared with laughter. He lay and listened to her for a few moments, then got out of bed, fetched his bathrobe from the kitchen and went upstairs to his own room.

THAT VERY AFTERNOON the Leader of the Council sat down and wrote a letter to the head of one of the biggest publishing houses in Stockholm.

"We have a resident in our care home, Sunnybank," he wrote, "who has been there for more than thirty years, and who long ago exhausted his financial allocation for board and care. For some time now this senior citizen has been devoting himself assiduously and continuously to writing. I dare not even mention his age. What he has produced are, according to his care assistant, stories of some kind. The Council is pleased to note that his writing seems to be what is keeping him alive, but at the same time has to take cognizance of the fact that local taxpayers are having to bear the cost not only of his writing materials but also of his prolonged life.

"If your publishing house were able to consider the publication and marketing of a book or books based on the original manuscripts of this gentleman in our care, it might produce a return which would cover a not inconsiderable proportion of his debt to the Council. There can be little argument that these stories, written under the circumstances described, constitute Council property. Their subject matter, again as reported by his care assistant, concerns characters from the past, their activities, maladies and, in a few cases, intimate relationships. Their lives seem mostly to lack aim or purpose, but that may well be irrelevant from a commercial perspective.

"Is the actual subject-matter of books of any significance?

"The Council's estimate is that this hitherto loss-making pensioner's output is around three hundred words a day, which is to say about three hundred pages a year. Would you be prepared to consider a contract between the Council and yourselves for a period of five years in the first instance? Would there be any possibility of an advance?

"In anticipation of a favorable reply, we remain, etc, etc," the Councilor signed off.

16

"Linda, have you ever seen a real conflagration, an entire house burn down?"

He was holding his pen between his new, healthy teeth, he had turned back several pages into what he had already written, and she was scraping the leftovers of his meal back onto the serving dish.

"We burned down the sheep shed," she replied. "But that was nothing much. The sheep had caught tuberculosis."

"So tuberculosis is still around?"

"The vet said it wasn't serious. But we burned the sheep shed anyway."

"You never know."

"No, you never know."

"Nothing can compare with a real conflagration," he said. "A conflagration combines the human and the natural world in equal measure. Even if it's a human who started it, the fire itself is an entirely natural phenomenon."

"I don't think I would want to experience it."

"At least one conflagration in a lifetime," he said. "I think we have a right to that much."

"So now there'll be fires, too!" said Linda.

"There's only one fire," he said. "It was the day before yesterday; that is the day before yesterday fifty-four years ago."

ROBERT MASER HAD driven his bus to Skellefteå. He had canceled their practice sessions for the last three days. He was singing the second voice of "My Grandfather's Drinking Cup" as he drove along, even though the roar of the engine drowned out his voice.

He sold a few yards of cloth, a couple of dresses, a suit and three pairs of pants in Finnfors and Krångfors. He would be spending the night at Persson's Guest House. And making two significant purchases.

That night Bertil came running over to Eva Marklund, his cheeks symmetrically blotched in agitation. "There's a fire!" he was shouting. "There's a fire!"

"Where?" said Eva.

"At Matilda Holmström's! The whole house is in flames!"

Lars Högström had come downstairs. "We'd better get over there," he said, "and see if there's anything we can do."

They half-ran, half-stumbled the mile or so there in the cold. Glancing up at the sky every once in a while they saw the Northern Lights for the first time that fall.

When they arrived Lars Högström said, "There's no sign of any fire here. You must have imagined it."

"It must have been the Northern Lights you saw," said Eva Marklund.

"Maybe I exaggerated slightly," said Bertil. "But I was convinced it was ablaze."

They were standing out on the road straining to see the house in the darkness. Everything was absolutely silent and still.

"Well, you never know," said Lars Högström. "I'll just make sure."

He disappeared into the house and came out a few moments later with the sheet music of Schubert's *Lieder*. "If Robert had been at home," he said, "he would have wanted us to save these."

"A real conflagration takes a bit of time to get started," said Bertil. "You don't see it right off."

"I'm freezing," said Eva. "I think I'll go back home."

"It's already burning in the wardrobe behind the dining room," said Bertil. "I'm sure of it. If it catches hold, you won't be freezing any more."

"Don't you think," said Lars Högström, "there might just be a slight smell of burning?"

They took a few paces up and down the road sniffing the air. And immediately concurred: they could detect the faint but unmistakable smell of smoke.

After that it was not long before the first flames were visible through the windows, first in the dining room and then in the kitchen. Soon the whole house was illuminated from within by the flames, the windowpanes shattered with little explosions, there were showers of sparks from the sawdust insulation in the walls, and the roof shingles began to curl and ignite. When the heat reached the three of them out on the road they moved back hesitantly and uncertainly without taking their eyes off the fire.

"I knew it!" said Bertil.

"Just think," said Eva, "how much tuberculosis is being burned up in there!"

"But what about Robert losing his home!" exclaimed Lars Högström.

An hour later there was practically nothing left of Matilda Holmström's house, except the stone foundations of the walls and smoldering lumps of charcoal and the iron stove glowing red-hot.

OVER THE NEXT few days Lars Högström got to hear from the children at school how the flames had been visible from Morken and Lillåberg and Björkås and Inreliden and how the smoke blew as far over as Åmträsk and Lillbäcken. You have to be careful with fire, he told them. Fire is the world putting itself at risk. Sparks and even tiny flames, or embers, whether white or red—all of them can be equally catastrophic.

Then he explained to them the word catastrophic.

So when Robert Maser got back from Skellefteå, he found himself homeless. He stood for a while in the half-light of dusk in front of the remains of what might have been his home, and then climbed into his bus and drove over to the Marklunds' house to say goodbye.

"I'll look for another uninhabited house," he said. "There are lots of them up here in Västerbotten. Abandoned crofts, unoccupied new buildings, empty huts."

"But you can stop for a bite to eat with us," said Eva Marklund.

It was that time of the evening. Lars Högström was already sitting in the kitchen, having taken his briefcase upstairs. Eva had cooked salted whitefish and made a white sauce. And there was fresh flatbread.

He found it difficult to refuse.

They ate for a while in solemn silence. All that could be heard was the crunching of bread between their teeth.

"It'll feel a bit deserted here without you," said Lars Högström after a while. "We need you in the village."

"It's not exactly over-populated here in Avabäck," Eva added.

"Is this fish just salted?" Robert Maser asked.

"I marinated it for several hours," Eva Marklund replied. "And I added a few spoonfuls of sugar to the salt."

"We could have gotten a lot further," said Lars Högström. "Especially with the German Romantics."

"If you drive north and then west along the Vindel River," Robert Maser asked, "do you eventually come to Ammarnäs?"

"Yes, you do."

"I've been lying awake at night," said Lars Högström, "wondering how to create a second voice for 'A King with Scepter I Have Been.' I think it could be extraordinarily beautiful."

"There must be something we could find in Avabäck," said Eva, "some empty property or other."

Bertil was sitting over by the door, needless to say.

"The only solution," he interjected, "is for him to move in here. That's what I thought all along."

"Well, now you say it . . ." said Eva.

"Actually," said Lars Högström, "I only really use the one room. If even that."

"If the meals were acceptable," said Eva.

"What I don't understand," said Robert Maser, "is how you can prepare the fish so there are no bones, yet the fish itself is still whole and apparently untouched."

And he added, "I've never, as far as I can remember, wanted to be any trouble to anyone. If my memory serves me right, I've kept myself to myself, kept a low profile. Other people may have let their lives expand and extend, but I've always been more of a second voice, the discreet lower part."

Matilda Holmström arrived a week later. The news had reached her of the house burning down. She put on high boots and went around kicking and poking at the ashes that in places were still warm. Eventually she found the metal ladle, the one Robert Maser had used when he had unsuccessfully tried his hand at making hash. It was twisted and the rivets securing the handle were a bit loose. She took it back with her to Adakgruvan as a souvenir.

17

So ROBERT MASER moved into Eva Marklund's house with all his worldly goods, those being the things he had bought in Skellefteå: a tuning fork and *The Household Cookbook*.

They drew lots for the rooms in what was known as the teacher's apartment. It was relatively unimportant to Lars Högström which room he had, now that he mostly slept in the bedroom downstairs.

And there was no doubt that Bertil was right in what he had said about their singing practice: it was much more convenient now that Robert Maser wasn't living out in the wilds, especially since the evenings had turned windier and more inclement and the snow was drifting onto the road and making it hard to see.

Thanks to the tuning fork their singing had taken on a new purity and confidence.

But when they looked at *The Household Cookbook* together, they were deeply disappointed. They stared in mourn-

ful incomprehension at the scanty and superficial instruc-
tions, the banal and unstimulating sentences: Soak 4 ozs of
pearl barley in 2 pints of water. Let it stand overnight. Boil
with 1 lb of lightly salted pork. Remove the meat when
cooked, but let the barley continue to simmer until soft.
Mince the pork and stir into the barley. Season with syrup,
vinegar and cloves.

After a moment or two of gloomy silence they both
broke into scornful laughter at the feeble prose, which was
completely lacking in inspiration and spirituality, and above
all manifested a staggering dearth of real experience.

THEY WOULD OFTEN read together in exactly that way, the
schoolteacher sitting at the table, the clothier standing behind
him, his right forearm supported on Lars Högström's shoulder and his left arm extended with his hand resting palm
downwards on the table. One evening they saw an article in
the newspaper or rather just a brief news item about the war
criminal Martin Bormann.

He had been sighted in Denmark, on Jylland. A warning
had been issued to the general public, since he was probably
still dangerous. He was posing as a farm laborer and had
been working on the sugar beet harvest near Skodsborg and
Bredebro over the summer; he was earning his living now at
various manual jobs. Even as a young man he had committed
acts of assault and murder. As a politician he had been
responsible for the deaths of millions. He had been con-
demned by the War Crimes Tribunal in Nuremburg to be

hanged. He was of average height, genial and good-humored in manner. His wife and children were still living in Germany and hoping for news of him.

"Sooner or later," said Lars Högström, "he'll get caught. That's the one thing I've learned in life, that no one ever gets away with things."

"If only," said Robert Maser, "the Communists had got the devil and tortured him to death and hacked him into little pieces."

"I DON'T UNDERSTAND your characters," said Linda.

"No one can understand them," he said as he went on writing. "Never ever."

She had made a serious attempt to find Avaberg mountain now. You could get everywhere by snow-scooter. She had approached from the Åmliden direction, and thought she had found Gammbrinken and Gårdbäcken and Lidträsket, maybe even seen Holkmyren, but she had still not found Avaberg.

"You'll have to try again," he said.

"Yes, I'll try again."

The minister came next, just as Liszt's *Preludes* were playing on the radio, in a recording by the Westphalia Symphony Orchestra. They stood listening, newspaper correspondent and minister. There was a half-empty cup of coffee on the table, and the last word in the notebook was incomplete. The minister had a bald and shiny pate, but hair hanging down over the collar of his black jacket. His clerical collar was half-hidden by a scarf, on which could be discerned the words Skellefteå Hockey Club.

"I'll never understand Franz Liszt," the minister said after a while. "In Berlioz and Brahms everything is profound and beautiful, but with Liszt it's all tawdry glitter and froth. When Martin Bormann wanted a signature tune for German radio, he chose Liszt. The first theme, which has strength and character in itself, he bungles like the worst variety-house musician you can imagine. The whole of that new German school of music were bunglers! And he was just a very ordinary person with bouffant hair, a fop from a madhouse! His music is like Beethoven symphonies played backwards. Musical whoremongering, spasmodic effects and inarticulate muddle! Brutal and clumsily composed contrasts!"

"Is this a pastoral talk?" he asked, his mind still on the article he was in the middle of writing.

"Yes, it is."

The cheap black plastic radio was vibrating with the volume of the music.

"Music," the minister went on, "is on the one hand reason and clarity of thought, conveyed by pitch, interval and time, and indicated by written notation. On the other hand it is illogical and absurd, consisting almost entirely of the most atrocious irrationality and emotionality, a repellent and indecent sentimentality.

"In Liszt, this dubious, not to say poisonous, sentimentality has completely taken over. Franz Liszt pretended to be seeking something he knew very well did not exist. He is the most vile, most disgusting charlatan in the history of music.

"And yet," the minister concluded, "I always have the distinct impression that there is something extremely significant concealed in Liszt's music. That the right performer would find its core and quintessence. It does have a demonic power. If the perfect interpreter could peel away all the superficiality, all the ornamentation and embellishment and dazzling and elegant cadences, then there's a deeper truth in there somewhere trying to get out. You can just detect it, in the second theme. A chaos of musical material that could lead anywhere. If I only understood Franz Liszt, then I might have something very important to say to my congregation. It's a great blessing to be able to speak the truth, and one should do it with caution and humility."

The minister had already opened the door on his way out as the newspaper correspondent asked, "Was that really a pastoral talk?"

"Yes," said the minister, "it was."

"SHOULDN'T WE BE able to understand people?" said Linda.

"Yes, of course," he said. "That would be best of all."

18

LATE ONE EVENING Lars Högström divulged his secret to Robert Maser; he was saving money. Not just generally, but for a very specific purpose. He was pleased that Robert Maser was now contributing thirty crowns a month to the housekeeping; indeed he was very grateful. He was not wasting a cent of his salary, apart from the odd piece of music he ordered. He was putting it all into his savings bank account, every bit that Eva didn't need.

"Eva? But you've agreed your board and lodging with Eva?"

Of course he had agreed a figure with Eva. But her needs sometimes went beyond the agreement, her needs were also their needs. The meals in this house were lavish, far superior to the norm in Avabäck.

"Yes," said Robert Maser, "yes, that's true."

"Have you ever given a thought to the flatbread and

the homemade butter from Gransjö and the bleak roe and smoked reindeer meat?"

Yes, Robert Maser had thought about the bleak roe.

IN WINTER AT that time there was a local study circle on psychology led by Mr. Bergqvist, the schoolteacher in Glommers-träsk, and there was a report on it, as there was on everything else, in the newspaper. The study guide was written by Dr. Alf Ahlberg. The life of the soul was, according to Plato, as Mr. Bergqvist said Dr. Ahlberg explained, the only real and true life.

Desperate attempts were being made in Adak to bore for water, but not a drop had yet been found even at a depth of 300 feet.

A boy in Granlund had shot two bull moose while out with a gun.

The continuous snowfall was causing difficulties for the lumber industry, and the chapel in Ragvaldsberg had been crushed by the weight of snow on its roof.

The Boliden Company was prospecting for uranium at various sites. The Swedish armed forces' need for atomic bombs could only increase.

A strong revivalist movement was growing in Holmsele. A dozen or so young people were opening themselves to God every evening. The revivalist meetings were led by Mr. Olofsson, the evangelist from Sorsele.

In the distant past, Eva reminded herself, she had sometimes gone to prayer meetings. But she no longer had anything in particular to pray for. So she wouldn't bother, she said.

A POSTCARD ARRIVED from Hällnäs, from Manfred. He wanted to thank her for having him. He was getting better and better by the day. There was no question of surgery yet. He asked for his greetings to be conveyed to everyone in Avabäck.

Two of the schoolchildren were sent to the sanitarium. They would receive tuition as well as treatment. Lars Högström added a few extra words to the morning prayers that they said in unison every day. He referred to them by name: Sigrid and Allan. "Release them, O merciful Lord, from their coughing and hemorrhaging."

One afternoon Bertil made a point of staying behind alone with Lars Högström in the classroom after the buses had taken the children home. The schoolteacher was practicing the next week's hymn on the harmonium, while outside one of the frequent snowstorms was raging.

"You ought to think about what you're doing," said Bertil. "I sometimes get the impression you don't really think about what you're doing at all."

"I do nothing else," said Lars Högström, "but think about what I'm doing. By the time you think, everything is already done. Lead us, Heavenly Father, lead us. I must find the right tempo. Guard us, guide us, keep us, feed us."

He was pressing the pedals and playing as he spoke.

"You take on too much," said Bertil. "You've taken on Eva. And now you've taken on this Robert Maser."

"If I were susceptible to anything," said Lars Högström, "then I'd be worried. Savior, breathe forgiveness o'er us. But I've got nothing to worry about."

The harmonium was hissing. Lars Högström had written to the Principal about it. The bellows would have to be patched or replaced.

"At this time of year," said Bertil, "it's probably okay. In winter when everything is frozen or buried under the snow. But come spring, you'll lose your grip."

"I can't lose my grip," Lars Högström replied. "Spirit of our Lord descending, fill our hearts with heavenly joy. I don't even need any grip."

"In the spring," Bertil went on, "the lake will thaw. And the ground frost will disappear, at least on the surface. And the snow will melt within a few days. And Avabäck will be one big river. Then you'll see!"

"Human life and the seasons," said Lars Högström, "are two different things. Love with every passion blending, pleasure that can never cloy."

He was half-singing and running his fingers over the keys and pumping the bellows as he was speaking.

"You're not listening to me," said Bertil. "You don't listen to anyone. You needn't think you can understand and anticipate everything just because you're a schoolteacher."

"I can never comprehend why you interfere," said Lars Högström. "You interfere in things that don't concern you. Thus provided, pardoned, guided, nothing can our peace destroy. You shouldn't keep interfering."

"I'm not interfering," said Bertil, making exactly equivalent deprecating gestures with both hands. "I'm already part of everything that goes on. I'm already here. I've been here from the beginning."

Lars Högström started again on Lead us, Heavenly Father, lead us.

BERTIL SUDDENLY TURNED up one morning in exactly the same way at Robert Maser's, who was sitting at his little table busily writing away in two notebooks.

"Is that your accounts you're doing?" he asked.

"I'm trying to understand," Robert Maser replied, "how much I'm actually selling. And stocktaking."

"It's not easy understanding things," said Bertil. "And no one knows whether it helps. As your understanding matures, it gets more self-contained."

"I like to imagine," said Robert Maser, "that these brief notes will help me. I make two columns, one for stock and one for income."

"Do you know yourself what you've got out there in the bus?"

"I have a good shot at it," said Maser. "When the thaw came I spent some time in the bus making notes."

"Do you know what gloria is, for instance?" asked Bertil. "And hopsack and twill? And brocade and cretonne and batiste and mull and canvas?"

"Gloria," Robert Maser replied, "is a form of Doxology, Greater or Lesser, and it can refer to the metrical form or musical setting."

"And the other types of fabric?"

"I must have known once. Since I'm a clothier."

"Have you ever wondered whether you're really needed here in Avabäck? We've never had a clothier before. If we'd been meant to have one here, there would have been one."

"I did ask about the road to Ammarnäs some time ago," Robert Maser replied. "You follow the Vindel River. But Mr. Högström and Mrs. Marklund persuaded me to stay."

"It must be a frightful burden," Bertil interposed, "to be phoney and superfluous. To create disorder and confusion just by your very existence. You never know where it might end."

"I find a lot of solace in music," said Robert Maser. "Singing practice with Mr. Högström. He can even play the harmonium in the school hall when we sing."

THE WEATHER WAS becoming more changeable. Some days you could see from the yellow edges and streaks in the snow where the frozen water was melting in the dikes around the fields in the marsh. Yet on other days more snow would fall. And the severe cold at nights caused the snow to freeze. The children were granted two days' vacation to go out on the frozen snow and collect pine cones, because the forests burned down by the war in Europe were to be replanted.

But before the dikes had started yellowing Bertil turned up at Eva Marklund's.

"I know what's going on between you and the school-teacher," he said. "Manfred might be dying," he pointed out. "He might be lying half dead in the sanitarium in Hällnäs."

"He's getting better every day," she said. "And he'll be happy enough just to improve."

"If you write to him," said Bertil, "give him my good wishes."

"I've already written," Eva replied. "I said there's nothing happening here and Avabäck is still completely iced up."

"That's good," said Bertil. "He probably wouldn't be able to take it if you wrote the truth."

"Truth," said Eva, "is so terribly black and white. It's dangerous to be a slave to truth. Truth is like tubercles."

She hadn't started reading the newspaper yet. The front page lay spread out under the lamp. "SOLAR PHENOMENON PRESAGES STORMS. In some places yesterday three suns were visible in the sky simultaneously. The phenomenon is thought to presage storms or change."

"I'm really quite astonished," said Bertil. "I never thought you would make yourself available."

"I've never made myself available," she said. "He was the one who made himself available."

She was standing at the sink chopping a turnip and carrots into little cubes. The water was boiling in the two pans on the stove.

"He's sharing himself," she said.

"I always thought," he said, "that if one fine day she were to make herself available, it would be to me. I was here first, before all the others. Except for Manfred."

Eva made no response to that.

"There oughtn't to be three of you here in this house," he continued. "Two is all right. Or four. But not three."

And he expatiated on the dangers of odd numbers, how everything that couldn't be divided equally represented a threat that could destroy mankind. It was the regular and homogeneous that created safety and security, anything ill-matched or unpaired was destructive and subversive and injurious. But four was okay.

He could mention that he had envisaged a bed under the stairs, in the outer lobby. He wouldn't need more than that, he would be quite happy. Then there would be four of them in the house. He didn't need heated rooms and home comforts. And then they would be two on each side of the kitchen table. It would be so much simpler for her to reckon up things in daily life, like how many potatoes to cook, how many plates to set out, the number of teaspoons of salt in the minced meat, everything in fact. And it would finally bring about the order and method essential for a respectable life, of which this house was in particular need.

But at that she put down the turnip she had in her hand and swung round and looked him straight in the eye and said that now he had gone too far. Her house, her and Manfred's house, was not just full but overfull. He should shut his mouth and be on his way. He had more than enough to do looking after his own affairs, lighting the fire in the school, fetching and delivering the mail, and to a limited extent keeping up with the doings of his fellow villagers.

IN WHIT-WEEK, Robert Maser went to Umeå. In one of the two music stores there he found a music book that had been printed in Leipzig in 1911. He blew the dust off and laid it on the sales desk, and together with the store owner muttered and mumbled his way through a few lines here and there.

"So you know German?"

"It seems so," said Robert Maser. "But doesn't everyone these days?"

"Well," said the store-owner, "it's mostly the educated classes. Army officers. And Mr. Hetta at the high school."

"The well," said Robert Maser, somewhat hesitantly, "has given me

refreshing drink,

now weariness

weighs me down no more.

I feel alive again

in the best of spirits,

with nothing obscuring my view."

"Yes," said the store-owner, "Siegmund really is a magnificent figure."

Robert Maser was leaning right forward, eagerly inhaling the store owner's breath.

"Your breath," he remarked, "has a faint but distinctive aroma. I can't help noticing it."

"It's nutmeg," said the store owner.

"Ah," said Robert Maser. "Nutmeg!"

"I've been eating offal," the store owner continued. "And offal is always spiced with nutmeg, to make it more interesting."

"Interest," said Robert Maser, only half-listening, "is the income from capital. If you've got any."

"That may well be, but I'm talking about offal," said the store owner. "And that's the lungs and heart and abdomen of a slaughtered animal. You mince them and spice them with onion and salt, and nutmeg, as I said, any amount of nutmeg."

"That's fascinating," said Robert Maser. "Quite fascinating."

"Then you fry the mixture and eat it with potatoes," the store owner expounded. "Offal is the cheapest and lowliest kind of food there is. Here in Umeå the smell of nutmeg is a real giveaway of a worthless business, not to mention poverty."

"It doesn't seem possible," Robert Maser objected, letting his eyes wander over the well-stocked shelves.

"Well, unfortunately, it is." Last year, the store owner confided, his wife had suddenly deserted him by dying. While she was alive she had contributed to the household income by playing the piano at choir practices. And sometimes at Free Church funerals. Besides, musical life was also dwindling. He was, to put it simply, dependent on society's musicality. And it was evident that society was developing in other directions, away from the musical and harmonious and artistic. He saw this constantly confirmed in his daily takings and accounts. So it was a real blessing if someone was actually going to buy these selections from *The Ring of the Nibelungen*. The book had lain untouched on his shelves ever since he took over the store.

"To tell you the truth," said Robert Maser, "I'm looking mainly for duets. I'll have to think about it."

"The less music," said the store owner, "the more offal. It's as simple as that."

"I would imagine the dish is rather tasty," Robert Maser contended.

"Strictly speaking," said the store owner, "there's no difference between offal and Swedish hash. Except for the pearl barley."

"Pearl barley?"

"Yes. Hash always has pearl barley in it."

"I find that hard to believe," Robert Maser said. "I've never had hash that had pearl barley in it."

"Well, I ought to know," said the store owner, raising his voice. "I was born here in Umeå! There has to be pearl barley in Norrland hash!"

Robert Maser closed the music book that was still lying on the counter.

"I don't think I'll take the Wagner after all," he said.

At the door he turned and asserted quite definitively, "Real Swedish hash, hash cooked upcountry, shouldn't contain a single grain of barley!"

EVERY OTHER WEDNESDAY she treated her two house guests to the most coveted meal of all, the dish they would have most liked to have every day, the food without equal. One of them mashed his potatoes, the other kept the yellowy-gray meat separate on his plate, and both of them had learned to cut the accompanying beetroot into small pieces perfectly proportioned to their mouthfuls for the ideal blend of taste, and they spread their flatbread thick with butter. They ate in complete silence, they made no mention on these Wednesdays of music or the wind or the snow, or of the undernourished and sickly children of Lillåberg and Niklastjärn, as they otherwise always did. Only the clink of cutlery against plates and the crunching of flatbread could be heard.

Only some time afterwards, when the last sensations of smell and taste had faded and Eva had finished washing the dishes and sat down at the table with them, were they able to say anything to one another.

They had begun to consider a musical evening at the school, duets and organ recitals for the benefit of some deserving cause, popular yet sublime and soulful songs by Swedish and German composers, a couple of chorales by Bach.

"No," said Eva. "You should be careful who you sing for. Here in this house you always know who you're singing for."

"But the general populace around here lives in indescribable spiritual poverty," said Lars Högström. "It's for their sake."

"I could never myself sing for the general public," said Eva Marklund.

From that evening onwards a delicate soprano could be heard blending with the two male voices, mostly singing melody.

19

THE COUNCIL TOOK two copies of the local newspaper for the care home. The elderly residents didn't read them, but the staff usually dipped into them during coffee breaks.

Linda would bring him the day's paper or that of the previous day, and he would cast a swift eye over the death notices. "When my article is finished," he said, "they won't need to print anything else for days."

"Do you get the news on the radio?" Linda asked. "The news you need?"

"There isn't any news," he said, making a dismissive gesture with his left hand to indicate his indifference.

No, it was easy to do without the so-called news, he went on, it all came round again, and if you felt the need for it, it was just a matter of helping yourself, the news was always there.

Then he might ask yet again, "What year is it?"

"2001," she would reply.

"Or 2002 or something," he said. "It's all the same to me."

"I have to tell you," Linda said, "that I've spoken to the Leader of the Council. I've told him about your writing. That you're busy compiling an article. No one else here in the Home writes articles. We shouldn't keep anything secret from the Council."

"You did right," he said. "We should speak about everything we know. You can never be too careful where the Council is concerned."

"I voted for him in the elections," said Linda.

"I voted in 1948," he said. "I wonder how long we keep our right to vote. I voted for Bertil Ohlin."

"You can never lose your right to vote," Linda said. "Everything else, but not your vote."

"If I should need to vote at any time," he said, "you'll help me, won't you?"

"I won't have to," she said. "The Council makes sure that votes are cast for all residents."

"They're soon going to start mining in Storliden," said Linda. "Copper and zinc. The Boliden Company. And any amount of iron ore."

"How much is there?"

"Two million tons. At least."

"But no gold?"

"Not in Storliden. But maybe in Norrliden."

"All chicken tastes like fish nowadays," he said of the

meal he had just had. "This chicken reminded me of the summer pike in Valviken."

"Chickens eat nothing but fish," Linda said. "That's why they taste of it."

"Our chickens used to eat oats and corn and worms and caterpillars. Is there nothing nowadays that's genuine and not artificial or falsified in some way?"

"I don't know," said Linda. "In the days when everything was genuine, I hadn't even been born."

And she went straight on to the question of Avaberg mountain. Could it be that Avaberg had existed in the past but didn't exist any longer?

"But you've got maps," he said. "You can see it on the maps."

"Well, yes," she admitted.

But it was rather strange that she always went wrong whenever she looked for Avaberg mountain. She wondered whether the maps were right. Maybe it had something to do with the compass? Or with the depressingly monotonous terrain? You never knew where one thing ended and another began.

"We should never give up," he said. "Everything has its time. But if we give up, then we have no time any more."

"No," she said. "I won't give up."

"But sometimes we need relaxation and amusement. Isn't there," he asked, with an facial expression he himself could have described, "any place for love in your life?"

Yes, she made love every Friday, for an hour or so after midnight. Sometimes longer, sometimes less. She had a boyfriend. His name was Michael and he lived in Renström. He was looking for iron ore, too. But his prospecting was in a totally different direction, further south on the other side of the Skellefteå River.

"BUT THAT MASER you're writing about," said Linda, "he's a weird guy. How old is he?"

"He doesn't know himself. But when he looks in his passport he sees he'll soon be forty-eight."

"But is he really the same person you wrote about at the beginning of the article?"

"He doesn't know himself."

"How can you say that?"

"Because the one follows from the other. I'm just writing the report, I don't have any responsibility. All reports include people who have been something completely different before."

"But how did he come to be in this area?"

"Have you never even heard folk talking about him?"

"I don't know. There was a very strange raincoat at home. So stiff it might have been made of chipboard or plywood."

"Really?"

"Apparently my grandfather had bought it from a mobile clothing merchant with a bus."

"Well, there you are. That was Maser," he said. "Robert Maser."

"I'd rather you got rid of him," Linda said.

"When a person has found his way into a report," he said, "he's hardly likely to be allowed out again."

BUT THE CONSTANT talk of searching and secrets and prospecting and exploration made him want to get on with his article:

In March Eva Marklund and Robert Maser became aware that the schoolteacher was reading the newspaper advertisements with great interest. But he always held the paper up in front of him so it was impossible for them to tell whether it was "Wanted" or "Lost" or "For sale" or "Announcements" that he was scanning.

And on the last day of April he seemed to have found what he was looking for. He went all the way over to Selma Grahn to use her telephone. When he came back both Eva and Mr. Maser could see that the object of his search was about to be his. The deed was done, and he didn't have to read the advertisement pages any longer.

"So you've settled your business?"

"Yes," said Lars Högström, "you could say so. It's exactly the kind of machine I've always dreamed of."

20

"THAT WASN'T WHAT I'd expected at all," said Eva.

"And I," said Robert Maser, "would have been more inclined to guess at a simple piano, with a wooden frame."

"Is that," said Eva, pointing, "really what you've been dreaming of?"

This prompted the school-teacher to say a few words about his childhood. The latter part had been pervaded by dreams of oxygen. When his grandmother had asked what he wanted for his birthday he had replied "Oxygen." And later sanitarium dreams had been of fresh air, and their most tangible expression dreams of motorcycles. The rushing wind

Motorcycle. Velocipede, propelled by internal-combustion engine. The engine, of one or two cylinders, is attached low in the center of the frame. The gas tank usually holds enough fuel for a journey of over 100 miles. Warm clothing of leather or similar material is essential for the motorcyclist. The motorized velocipede is an excellent mode of transport for the bold and enterprising.

would impel unimaginable quantities of oxygen down his

throat and windpipe and lungs, and with streaming hair and his eyes and mouth wide-open and his chest expanded by the forces of nature, he would sate all his craving for air with the aid of a motorcycle.

"So that's probably why," he said.

"But you're cured," said Eva. "You're even immune."

"Immunity," said Lars Högström, "has no influence over dreams and emotions."

"Manfred," Eva recalled, "often used to talk about a horse that could gallop at the speed of lightning. If he could ever afford it."

"This is fifteen horsepower," said Lars Högström. "It hasn't got a speedometer, but it can do over sixty miles an hour. It's called a Diamond."

And there was the name in gold lettering on the newly painted black gas tank.

"A motorcycle," said Robert Maser, "is not just a mode of conveyance but also an instrument for conquering the world."

"It's been completely overhauled," Lars Högström said. "It took part in the war."

Then he sat astride the machine, adjusted his position and kicked the start pedal. On the fourth attempt the engine throbbed into life. And he twisted the throttle so that the sound of the engine could be heard and enjoyed at high revs as well as low. As he eased the choke back with his thumb he commented, "When it's actually moving it has a pleasanter, more muffled sound to it."

"It sounds lovely," said Eva.

"It's a beauty," said Robert Maser.

"The engine," said Lars Högström, "is made in Dresden. But the whole bike is assembled at the Diamond Works in Saxony."

"That means nothing to me," said Robert Maser.

"But somehow," said Eva Marklund, "it's found its way right up here to Avabäck."

"It was imported by Martin Carstedt in Kristineberg and it weighs three hundred pounds," Lars Högström said as he patted the leather cushion fastened to the luggage rack. "It's designed to take passengers," he said, with a look at Eva.

"No," she said, "it would be improper. And shameful. On such a monster."

Then he squeezed the big black rubber bulb so they also got to hear the horn.

BY THE STEPS, between there and Robert Maser's bus, where Eva used to throw out the dishwater, the grass was already very high. And now Bertil popped up out of it and sauntered over to the motorcycle. He bent down to inspect the engine.

"The flanges are small for a 500cc bike," he said. "And the carburetor is a bit antiquated, it has to be primed. The new downdraft carburetors let it idle at much lower revs."

To which he added, "The British make much more modern machines."

"German quality," said Lars Högström. "I could have bought a British bike, a Terrot. But I wanted a German one."

"It was the British who won the war," Bertil pointed out.

"What war?" said Robert Maser.

"German technology," said Lars Högström, "is the best in the world."

"If you'd bought a car," said Bertil, "we could have all four gone out together."

But he was corrected by the schoolmaster: there was no bond that united them in a way that would make the expression "all four" appropriate. Four wasn't even a particularly sacred number. He could think of many other numbers, but there could never be any question of four.

Robert Maser went off into his still well-stocked, perhaps inexhaustible, bus and was gone for some minutes. When he came back he was carrying the precise clothes that were needed: two pairs of pants, two jackets, two caps, two pairs of boots, and all in a dark-brown material that might have been leather or rubber or something in-between.

So they were equipped for whatever journeys and adventures might turn up.

"WERE THERE REALLY motorcycles at that time?" Linda asked.

"That time? What time?"

"The time you're writing about, the time in the article."

"More or less everything has always existed," he said. "It's just their manifestations that shift and change in minor ways."

"This article you're compiling, that hasn't always existed."

"No," he admitted after a few moments' thought. "A few odds and ends must be created out of nothingness."

SPEAKING OF WHICH, he needed a new notebook. And he'd like a couple of pens with finer points. His sight was getting better and sharper all the time, and with a finer point he would be able to write more neatly and economically.

"And," he said, "could you get me a large sheet of paper? A yard or so wide and a couple of yards long. And a box of colored crayons."

Linda was busy changing the sheets on his bed. She stood up, holding the pillow against her chest.

"I'll have to ask someone about that," she eventually replied. "The manageress. Or the Council Leader."

"Do you think they would like to read the article itself?"

"No."

"The Council Leader has already forgotten me. And the manageress doesn't know who I am."

"She often asks how you're getting on. And there isn't a sparrow that falls to the ground without the Leader of the Council knowing of it."

"White paper," he said. "And those hard, round crayons."

THE COUNCIL LEADER certainly had not forgotten him. In a brief reminder to the head of the publishing house in Stockholm he wrote that he had been awaiting a reply to his previous letter for some long time, and he enclosed a copy

of same. "Our district may be spread out and sparsely populated," he wrote, "but even in the most desolate parts of the
country decisions have to be taken and actions put into effect.
Perhaps in my previous communication I did not make suffi-
ciently clear the deep sense of responsibility I feel for every
single person entrusted to my care."

21

THERE ARE TWO roads to Lillåberg: the old road that goes around the lake past Riskläppen and over the bridge beyond Långmyrliden and ends by the round barn in Lillåberg, and the new road that was built by the civil defense workers in the thirties, that goes straight across Långmyren moor itself.

They took the old road. It was their first trip. Lars Högström leaned his back into the cushioned support provided by Robert Maser's solid, rotund stomach. They paused at Riskläppsudden and Robert Maser produced from his ruck-sack the sandwiches that Eva had made for them. As they ate, he said, "It's strange, but I keep thinking of Mecklenburg. I don't know what the countryside looks like in Mecklenburg, I don't even know whether I've ever been there. But as soon as I sit on your Diamond it feels as if I remember Mecklenburg."

"Well, in June," said Lars Högström, "in the first warmth of summer, Norrland could be anywhere and be called anything."

The mosquitoes were not yet in evidence, and they stood peacefully looking out over the lake. Eva had put slices of preserved meat in the sandwiches covered with finely chopped parsley.

"I suppose there aren't such things," said Robert Maser, "as three-seater motorbikes?"

"No, there aren't."

"How far have we come?"

"Twenty miles or so. We'll be there in under an hour."

"There are sidecars," Robert Maser persisted. "The third person could travel in the sidecar."

"And if I had to ride alone at any time," Lars Högström responded, "what would I do with the sidecar?"

"But her presence might give an added enhancement to the trip," said Robert Maser.

"Yes," Lars Högström admitted, "she's a wonderful person."

IN LILLÅBERG THEY parked the motorbike in the farmyard, took off their caps and unfastened their stiff, shiny jackets. Beyond the pine forest to the west they could see Trollberg Mountain and Klåvaberg Mountain. There was a currant bush at the corner of the house, already green.

Rachel of Lillåberg came out onto the steps, wearing a bonnet on her head and a brown shawl across her shoulders. They went over to her to exchange greetings and introduce themselves. But they didn't state their business yet.

"I know who you are," said Rachel. "We tend not to talk about who we are in these parts."

"We're just out for a ride on the motorbike," said Robert Maser.

"I can see that."

"You've already planted your potatoes," said Lars Högström. "The first shoots are almost visible."

"I had some seed potatoes left," said Rachel. "Mostly almond potatoes but also some pinks and some Finnish reds. Since Uno died I always have a lot of things left over."

So they chatted for a while about potatoes, their varieties and diseases and uses. Lars Högström could even say a few words about soils and fertilizers and storage and yields.

"But I had two barrels go rotten this winter," said Rachel. "A person living alone can't eat unlimited quantities of potatoes."

"Even the great German writer Goethe penned a song in praise of the potato," Lars Högström said.

"It's unimaginably hard being left on your own," said Rachel.

"There's a country that's more or less just one big potato field," said Robert Maser. "It's called Mecklenburg."

"To southerners, potatoes are only one root crop among many," said Lars Högström. "They mostly fry them."

"Uno," said Rachel, "while he was alive, he could eat just about any amount of potatoes."

"We should have come to express our condolences," said Robert Maser.

"You don't start up a motorcycle for a thing like that," said Rachel.

"I saw it in the paper," said Lars Högström. "It was just after I'd taken up my post. I've included Lillåberg in our prayers."

At last she asked, "Can I offer you anything?"

A glass of water was all they could think of. The water up here in Lillåberg was renowned for miles; they wouldn't mind stepping into the kitchen and trying the water. Didn't it come up under its own pressure from the spring at Lillmyrkällan?

Yes, it was natural pressure. Uno had dug the pipeline.

They sat down at the kitchen table, sipping the water. Despite the warmth outside Rachel had the stove going. They unzipped their motorcycle boots.

"I know it tastes of iron at this time of year," she said. "But we don't notice it any more, Uno and me."

Eventually Lars Högström plucked up the courage to mention their business: presumably hash was made in Lillåberg?

"The hash from here," Robert Maser explained, "has been drawn to our attention."

Yes, of course. She had her hash. Though really it was Uno's hash. She herself preferred potted pork or ordinary haslet or liver stew. But for Uno's sake she had made hash from all the offal and the heads and flanks.

"That's a lot," said Lars Högström.

"For a person living alone," said Rachel, "it's quite absurd."

Then Lars Högström ventured, "I suppose it wouldn't be possible to try a little?"

Why, yes, of course! Anyone who wanted to taste hash could always come to her! And she had potatoes on the stove right now, and she'd put on enough to have some left over for the pig. She could give them cold hash cut into slices as well as hot hash with onions and black pepper. She was only too glad to have it eaten up, she could feed any number of school-teachers and clothiers with hash.

"So you know all about us?" said Robert Maser.

"Everyone knows," she said, "who you are."

"Well, thanks," said Lars Högström. "We'd love to try it."

They were at the kitchen table for some time. They mashed or chopped the hot hash with the almond potatoes, they put the cold slices on flatbread. The beetroot smelled a bit vinegary. Rachel stood at the stove. She would warm up a few slices of meat for herself later. They stopped from time to time to praise her hash, telling her it was exactly the sort of hash they had been expecting in Lillåberg, so full-flavored, so redolent of bone-marrow and offal, so firmly set and finely minced.

"What makes it so gray and muddy-looking," said Rachel, "is the tongue. Uno always wanted tongue in it, pig's tongue as well as calf's tongue."

"I'm sure he was absolutely right," Robert Maser said.

"Tongue," said Lars Högström, "has a very special quality. Hash made with tongue is obviously richer than hash in which the head is not represented at all."

But the worst thing about it was, she said, that she would be making Uno's hash for the rest of her life. That was the least she could do for him. What she had put in front of them now was last year's hash, and come the fall she would be making the same hash in the same quantity. It would be unthinkable to do anything else. She knew Uno was gone for ever, but that couldn't be helped. The cellar would slowly be filled up with last year's hash and the year before's and the year before that and with all the years of hash up to her death. There was nothing she could do about it.

"Hash like this," said Lars Högström, "will keep indefinitely."

"Life's just like that," Rachel concluded.

"Yes," Robert Maser agreed. "We have our obligations."

"Was it your Uno who carved the wooden moose out along the new road?" Lars Högström asked.

"Yes, that was Uno."

"YOU'RE LIVING AT Eva Marklund's, aren't you? She presumably has hash?"

"Yes, of course! She was the one who introduced us to it. Her hash is outstanding."

"So it's better than this?"

"Not better but different. We've come to realize that no one hash is like any other. There are as many types of hash as there are people. At least, we

> **Wooden moose**. Life-size figures representing moose, usually carved from six or seven conjoined pieces of wood.
>
> The majority of wooden moose in the country can be found in central and northern Sweden, often by the roadside or in private gardens.
>
> There is some controversy about the significance of the wooden moose in primitive or pastoral cults.
>
> See Joel 1:20: "The beasts of the field cry also unto thee".

suspect that to be the case. We're still at the beginning of our research."

"Our modest desire," said Robert Maser, "is to carry out a provisional survey."

Rachel stood at the stove watching them as they ate. Once or twice she went over to the table and moved the carrots and the china dish decorated with blue flowers nearer to their plates. "Don't stand on ceremony," she said. "It's such a long time since I had the chance to serve a meal to anyone."

FINALLY LARS HÖGSTRÖM clasped his hands in front of his chest and thanked the Lord for the gifts they had received. And Robert Maser rose to his feet and zipped up the legs of his close-fitting pants and gave a short speech of gratitude to Rachel for her hospitality, praising the hash and also the splendid almond potatoes, the beautifully baked flatbread and the full-cream milk. He actually stood to attention as he spoke. But he didn't mention the beetroot.

Before they left, Rachel brought up five jars of potted hash from the cellar. Robert Maser put them carefully in his rucksack where Eva's sandwiches had been.

"Since you gentlemen are so kind as to have expressed your appreciation of it," she said.

They took the new road this time. They made a brief stop at the crossroads where the wooden moose was. "He was a skillful guy," said Robert Maser. "That moose was done with great sensitivity."

"We ought to come over here and give it a coat of tar," Lars

Högström said. "To protect it and save it for future generations."

Back home in Avabäck they put the hash in Eva's kitchen. She had washed the bed linen that day, and four pillowcases that Robert Maser had given her had fallen apart and dissolved in the lye.

When she saw the jars she stood eyeing them for a moment, then said, "So, my hash isn't good enough any more."

"You mustn't take it like that," said Lars Högström. "Rachel in Lillåberg just wanted to please us. And if you ever want a day off from cooking . . ."

"I wouldn't have expected this," Eva said. "I can't say I don't feel hurt."

And there was Bertil sitting by the door all of a sudden and offering his opinion: "Yes, it has to be said, it's a bit of a cheek and an insult."

"What were we to do?" said Robert Maser. "Rachel forced her hash on us."

"She put it in our rucksack herself," said Lars Högström.

"Even so," said Eva.

"There's nothing else for it," said Bertil, "but for me to take charge of the pots. And make sure no one sees them again. You have to be as tactful as a saint about hash. Your own and other people's."

That evening Lars Högström made his first notes about these trips and the investigations that were to occupy him and Robert Maser for a whole summer.

WHEN LINDA BROUGHT the big sheet of white paper and the box of colored crayons to the reclusive writer in the care home, he was sitting hunched up in bed, his feet on the bedcovers and his chin supported on his knees. He was listening to the radio. She sat down beside him.

It was a man called something like Skinnarmo. He was talking about the North Pole, which he had made an attempt to reach. The North Pole is one of two places where the Earth stands still. It is a harsh and pitiless environment. You have to take two months' supplies by sledge. You might have to shoot a polar bear in self-defense. The polar bear has no one to blame but itself. The footprint of a polar bear is as big as the lid of a well. Your breath freezes immediately: you actually exhale ice. Out on the ice your main thought is of death. It can take half an hour to travel a hundred yards. The walls of ice can be twenty to twenty-five feet high. All the time you're sure you've chosen the wrong route. Man has always endeavored to find the North Pole. Pythias, Vasco da Gama, Magellan, Willoughby, Barents. All those who died for the North Pole died in vain. Whiteness consists of gray, blue and possibly white. The speaker's voice was frail and hoarse and tense. The ice rumbles and groans continuously.

How many people have made it to the North Pole so far?

Hundreds of thousands.

When it was over Linda said, "But you wonder what it is he's trying to discover."

"He's just exploring. He's an explorer. In the broadest sense."

"Though he must have a good idea himself," said Linda, "what it is he's looking for."

"It's probably impossible to know in advance."

"Nobody can travel around like that without having something particular in mind."

"He probably has a hammer and a pickaxe and cuts chips out of the ice. You never know."

Then he said, "Ah, that paper's fine, big enough and good quality. You obviously listen to what people say to you. And they were exactly the sort of crayons I meant. Crayola."

22

WHEN HE WAS alone again he unrolled the white paper on the floor and stuck it down on the vinyl floor-covering with the tape that Linda had bought on her own initiative. Then he went to bed. On the radio Barbara Hendricks was singing the Countess's recitative and aria from the third act of *The Marriage of Figaro*.

In the morning, when he had eaten the oatmeal Niklas brought him, he set to work.

"I won't say anything," Niklas had said.

"About what?"

"The manageress wouldn't like that," he said, pointing to the paper and the crayons. "It's not part of the program."

"What program?"

"The Council's. The Council's budget program."

"No one needs to know. By the time you bring the mutton with dill sauce and rice I'll have finished and cleared it away."

"I won't say anything, anyway," said Niklas.

First of all he took his pen and drew the most important lines: the roads and paths and the river and the lake beaches and main dikes. He marked the site of mountains and springs and he wrote in the most significant names. Then he picked up the colored crayons, supporting himself on his left leg as he knelt so that his right hand could move freely and easily, and used the three green ones to put in a background of forest and bogs and tiny little fields, with here and there some fir scrub and single pines and yellowing birch. He made the water deep blue with touches of black, with a hint of black also in the wettest places, in the swamps and pools and mud.

Then he selected the best red, carmine, and put in the human habitation, all the houses he had seen and remembered or that he had heard mentioned and described, and he wrote their names in the same vivid blood-red color: Avabäck, Inreliden, Lillåberg, Kullmyrliden, Ristjöln, Åmträsk, Björknäset, Lakaberg, Finnträsk, Granträskliden, Nyklinten, Kläppmyrliden, Burheden, Morken, Lillsjöliden, Gammbrinken, Ensamheten, Lillvattnet and Granbergsliden. He even restored Matilda Holmström's burned down house. He joined together the houses and villages and isolated crofts and cultivated fields with roads and paths and bridges and footbridges in bright chrome yellow, and drew the boat jetties and mailboxes and the Lycksele bus route across the map with the ochre-colored crayon. In the bottom right-hand corner he indicated with an arrow the road that went to the sanitarium in Hällnäs.

He sketched Klåvaberg mountain, no longer bare but covered with new forest, yellowy-green and prettily rounded with even slopes on all sides.

And Oxkall spring and Hömyrbäck brook and Riskläppen hill and Teresias spring were also allocated their individual names and colors.

But right in the center he put Avaberg mountain. He let it rise up out of Gårdbäck moor and Avabäck moor with its rugged slopes to the south and west and steep cliff and sheer faces to north and east. He let mosses and lichens glint on the boulders and bedrock, he placed dead pines and rusty fox traps in their rightful positions and indicated with white dots the sites where prehistoric stone slabs still lay exposed and bare. Along the south side he let the Avabäck stream rage as in the spring thaw, as if it was the Vindel river at the Vormsele falls, splashing its blue-white water over the stones and heather and dwarf birch, even onto the potato field above Eva Marklund's house. He used a fish symbol to denote the little cave where the trout congregated, at the bottom of the hill.

No, nothing was omitted on this map, everything was there just as it had been created.

He didn't take a rest, it wasn't necessary, he was crawling slowly forward over the paper pushing the box of crayons ahead of him, occasionally chewing off a few flakes of the colors he liked best and had been attached to as a child, umber and carbon black. He didn't even slow down or stop when he came to his own house and his own forest, all that had once belonged to him.

When Niklas brought the mutton with dill sauce and rice and the little bowl of semolina pudding, the whole map was finished and rolled up. He had stood it between the wardrobe and the window, next to the radiator.

So NOW HE could get back to his notebook:

They made twenty-three trips that summer, Robert Maser and Lars Högström.

Sometimes Robert Maser would say, "You're driving too fast! I'm scared!"

Or more precisely: he shouted it into the headwind and engine noise and crunch of gravel on the road. But Lars Högström would shout back, "Nothing can happen to me! So nothing can happen to you! Not while you're sitting behind me!"

"I suspect I'm a coward!" Robert Maser bellowed. "Though I'm not sure!"

VERY SOON EVERYONE knew who they were, as well as what they were doing.

"Aha, so you're the two who're riding around sampling our hash," people said. "We've heard about you. Some folks just ride around at random with no object in mind."

"Yes," they said. "We're glad we've discovered hash."

And in every house or isolated croft they came to they would be greeted with: "It's an honor for us for you to have come this far."

"We've heard so much about your hash," they would reply. "It would have been an indefensible omission, almost a crime, not to have come here."

On a few occasions Bertil was there before them. Lars Högström asked, "How did you get here? And how did you know it was here you should come?"

"Everyone knows. Where you're going and why you're going. So how could I not know?"

"But what are you up to?"

"I'm only trying to keep an eye on things. Just generally. That's as big a responsibility as looking for something in particular," he said.

"Anyway, if you know anything about hash, it's easy enough to work out the routes you'll take."

GERDA AT INRELIDEN didn't cook hash any more. "No," she said, "who should I cook it for? A widow sitting eating hash, I can't imagine anything more unnatural. Or disgusting."

"But what do you do with all that meat now the flanks and heads and knuckles?"

"I would rather bury it than turn it into hash," she said. "When you've had a husband like Jakob and lost him, you don't make hash any more."

Out in the yard there were some splendid raspberry canes, the fruit almost ripe. She invited them to try some. "They came from Isabella Stenlund's bushes," she said. "They're sweeter than any others."

But Lars Högström and Robert Maser didn't want to

venture upon anything they considered irrelevant or distracting. They weren't hungry, it wasn't because of ordinary hunger that they had asked about her hash.

"Mind you, I've got a couple of pots I had from Isabella," she said. "I'll never open them for myself. But that doesn't stop me offering them to others."

"Thank you," said Lars Högström.

"That would certainly be something," said Robert Maser.

They sat on the steps in front of the house. The yard before them was completely bare, the grass poor and sparse. The rowan blossom was already fading, the willowherb over by the barn just coming out. She had sliced the hash into little pieces and put them on flatbread.

"Ah," Robert Maser said, "it's good. We can certainly approve that."

"But you can taste that someone else has cooked it," said Lars Högström. "It gives a definite impression of being hash from elsewhere."

"Of course," said Gerda. "Homemade is always different. Everything you cook yourself has your own mark on it. Hash that's come as a gift can never be like your own."

"It's not a criticism," Robert Maser said. "In no way to be taken as a censure of another person's hash."

"In fact we would be grateful," said Lars Högström, "if you would pass on our warmest greetings to Isabella Stenlund."

IN MORKEN THEY got to try game hash. Lots of people had talked about it. No one had known how it was made. "If only grandma had been alive!" they all said. "Or our great aunt!"

It was one Saturday afternoon. The family at Morken were out in their yard, between the main steps and the shed, waiting for them. Or rather, looking as if they were waiting for them. Perhaps they always stood outside like that on Saturday afternoons.

Yes, they had heard the tasters were on their way. They were prepared. Usually this was hash that was made in the winter. It was winter hash. You had to respect the seasons and their path across the earth. It was no coincidence that animal pelts were fit for use only during the four winters and birds' eggs available only in the summer. But they had heard that this visit was about hash, which really belonged to fall and winter, so they had made winter hash in the middle of summer. It was in the kitchen waiting for them now. It had been in the cold-store to set, in so far as game hash can set. It could never be cut into such neat slices as pork hash and other tame hash. Would the gentlemen like to know the recipe before they tried it?

"Yes, please," said Lars Högström, extracting his notebook from his inside pocket.

You shoot fifteen squirrels and flay and gut them. Then a doe hare. You boil them whole with coarse salt. When it's all cooked and tender you pound the boned meat in a mortar. Then boil up the stock and add the meat. If you want the hash to set so it can be sliced, you add a drop of the glue you've made from cows' hooves.

That's all there is to it.

Yes, it had a strong gamey flavor. It was dark brown in color. The smell of glue was also perceptible. The family stood watching in absolute silence as they ate.

"I shot six of the squirrels," said one of the boys. "I aim for their ears."

"Yes," said Lars Högström, "that's right, to go for the ears."

"It has an extremely potent flavor," said Robert Maser.

"You can never mistake game," said Lars Högström. "The taste is quite uncivilized, if you'll allow the expression. That flavor doesn't exist in the cities, hardly even in Lycksele or Malå or Norsjö."

"I can't say," Robert Maser remarked, "that it puts me in mind of anything in particular."

"But you like the strong taste?" Lars Högström asked him.

"Yes," Robert Maser reluctantly admitted. "It's an extraordinary taste."

And they were shown the meat mortar, a hollowed-out log, and the pestle, made of birch. Lars Högström measured the diameter with a folding ruler they lent him: twenty inches.

Then Lars Högström made a speech to the family. He owed it to them after all the trouble they had gone to. He had finished his hash, Robert Maser stood ready to go, and outside the smell of their motorcycle had spread right across the yard. "One may forget everything," he said, "but never the game hash in Morken."

ONE SUNDAY THEY lost their way and found themselves up in Raggsjö near the border with Lapland. They had gone wrong on the small roads and were way off their map. They rode slowly up Raggsjöliden hill past the mission house, the four milk-stands and the two chicken sheds and all the barns and the drying-house for producer-gas coke, and finally they rode up to Andreas Lindgren's house. They stood the Diamond, their motorbike, beneath the rowan tree above the house. They stood for a moment on the steps to admire the view: a continuous vista of lakes and mountains, maybe even the distant sea the furthest blue line could well be the Gulf of Bothnia. But no sign of any people.

Then in the kitchen they found a boy, sitting by the wood-box with a piece of white cardboard and a stump of black crayon in his hand. "I'm trying to draw Gösta Berling," he said without looking up. "I'm reading *Gösta Berling's Saga* in the evenings, and I want to know what he actually looked like."

"Are you at home on your own?"

Yes, he was the only one at home. His brothers, Rolf and Göran, had cycled over to Kvarnåsen to watch a seaplane land on the lake. And his parents had gone to the cemeteries, both cemeteries, to tend the graves.

He put down the crayon and straightened up. He had a strangely emaciated and elongated appearance, as if he had been stretched on a rack.

"We don't want to intrude," Robert Maser said.

"We've got such an incredible number of graves," the boy said. He spoke very slowly, as if he were taking a breath between each word.

In fact as far as graves were concerned, his family could compete with more or less any family you might like to name. His uncles and aunts on both sides and both sets of grandparents and other relations had died at a younger age and in greater numbers than was normal. If it wasn't consumption it was cancer and now recently heart failure of various kinds. And they had been buried one after another in two different churchyards in Norsjö, and in the summertime all these graves had to be tended just as much as the potato field and the cabbage patch.

"What's your name?" Lars Högström asked.

"I'm Torgny. Torgny Lindgren."

"And why can't you go and watch the plane landing on the lake?"

"I'm not really well enough. I've got a touch of consumption. Otherwise I'd have loved to go and see it. Aren't you afraid of getting infected?"

"No," said Robert Maser. "We're immune."

The two visitors had sat themselves down at the kitchen table, which is what they had taken to doing wherever they went, and through the window they could see the currant bushes and the raspberry patch and the dark red clusters of berries hanging heavily on the bushes.

"We're going to press the redcurrants later in the week and make jelly," the boy volunteered.

On the table lay a bobbin and a hand-forged pair of scissors. Robert Maser picked them up to look at them.

"We're going to set up a loom," said the boy. "When winter comes we'll be weaving rugs."

"You've probably heard about us," said Lars Högström. "We go around on our motorbike, the Diamond, here in the hinterland of Västerbotten. We're carrying out a survey of the state of affairs in certain respects."

No, as far as he knew no one had heard of them here in Raggsjö. Two men riding a motorbike and investigating something or other? No, he was sure that wasn't anything that was known or discussed in his village. Had it been in the local paper?

No, not yet.

"When you grow up," said Robert Maser, "you could ride a motorbike too."

Well, that was far from certain. The fact was that he would never grow up. Everyone was more or less agreed on that. So far he only had patches on the lungs and enlargement of the glands. But that was how it had started for most of those who had ended up in the graves he had mentioned. No, there would be no motorbike for him. And no plane, either, as he had said.

"No child should be as gloomy and negative as that," Lars Högström said. "A child should be looking forward to life's great adventures."

"And nowadays," said Robert Maser, "new medicines and new treatments are being discovered all the time."

"Don't misunderstand me," the boy said. "I'm not complaining. No, on the contrary, I'm very grateful."

He was grateful, he explained, that he wouldn't have to reach adulthood. He would avoid military service, and he wouldn't even have to be rejected as unfit. He would never be at the beck and call of any forest warden or manager or foreman. He would never have to be stuck alone in the forest eating dried pike. No one would ever expect to be maintained by him. There wouldn't be time for him to sit at many deathbeds. And he would never need to wear a broad-brimmed hat. He would avoid dying of cancer. No, they mustn't think he was complaining. And besides, he sometimes felt such a fierce and crazy joy, not to say bliss, just to be alive, that it really was best that he should never grow up, because no one could gauge or predict what a person with such a mentality might develop into.

"But here in Raggsjö," he said, "consumption is almost eradicated. When I'm gone, everyone will be healthy."

"Do you never get sad and cry?" Lars Högström asked.

"We northerners from Västerbotten let our tears out through our navels," he replied. "So no one notices."

Then he asked, "Do you gentlemen think Gösta Berling could possibly have had a squint?"

"Gösta Berling didn't really exist," Lars Högström said. "He's only fiction. A character in Selma Lagerlöf's book."

"That doesn't make any difference," the boy said.

Robert Maser's little finger had caught in the bobbin. He shook it free with a sudden flick and declared, "Jesus said, Suffer the little children to come unto me."

"The Lord is my shepherd," Lars Högström added.

"Though I walk through the valley of the shadow of death, I will fear no evil, for thou art with me, thy rod and thy staff they comfort me."

"That may well be so," said the slight yet tall thin boy, "though we haven't come to any absolute certainty about God and Jesus. Not in the village nor in our family. On my mother's side we mostly believe only in God, but on my father's side from here in Raggsjö we believe more in Jesus Christ. There are lots of people who don't believe in anything in particular. My parents are sometimes believers, sometimes not. So we'll have to see."

Then he went on to ask a question: "But Gösta Berling was a priest and a believer, wasn't he?"

"Yes," said Lars Högström. "Yes, he was."

"BUT WHEN YOU reach adulthood," Lars Högström continued, "if you allow yourself to grow up, then you can choose for yourself the kind of life you want, you're free to seek out the best and most important and most satisfying things in life. A purposeful search like that is beyond the scope of a child. A sense of vocation."

"We thought we remembered," said Robert Maser, "that someone a long time ago mentioned a special Raggsjö hash. Hash with a particularly light and fresh taste."

"It's a shame," said Lars Högström, "that your mother has gone out to the family graves. Otherwise we could have tasted a morsel. But of course we realize the graves have to be tended."

Well, yes, came the acknowledgment from the wood-box, you might say there was a Raggsjö hash. Though actually it was more complex than that. Strictly speaking Raggsjö was an agglomeration of a number of smaller villages, and each of them had its own hash with its own characteristics and variations. Gårdbäck hash and Brinken hash and Kläppen hash were basically the same as Raggsjö hash despite their minor differences. But of course a tasting for the gentlemen could be arranged. Though only the hash: they would have to imagine whatever accompaniments there should be, because at the moment all the house could offer was a small sample of the hash itself.

"Our gratitude would be beyond measure," said Lars Högström.

So the boy took two plates from the cupboard above the sink, opened the trapdoor of the cold-store under the floor, and climbed down the narrow steps, puffing and panting laboriously. They could hear his wheezing and the scrape of knife against china down in the cellar. When he came back up there were two thin slices of hash on each plate. He put them before his guests and produced a fork each from the top drawer by the sink.

The pattern on the plates was clearly visible through the hash, so pure and clear was it: Vines, from Gävle China Factory. And the taste was unusually straightforward and easily defined, a distinct acidity but above all an unambiguous aroma of meat. Put simply, it consisted of well-cooked meat fibers separated and surrounded by an aspic as clear as glass.

"Sublime," Lars Högström sighed.

"We usually whisk a couple of egg whites into the simmering broth," the boy said, "then we strain it through a colander and muslin. And the liquid looks like water."

"If a book were to be written," said Robert Maser, "could it just be called Raggsjö hash?"

"A book? About our hash?"

"Yes."

"Of course. Raggsjö hash. And we add a couple of tablespoons of vinegar at the end."

It was Lars Högström who proposed that they sing a song for the poor lonely lad in Andreas Lindgren's kitchen, to express their thanks for the hash and bring a little happiness into his life and some slight comfort. No, perhaps not comfort, he didn't need that, but a memory, an experience. They chose "All Alone Was I, and Alone Came He," in Rangström's setting. They stood on either side of the kitchen table, at first with their fingertips on the table. The arrangement was their own, with repeats of Runeberg's lines in couplets. Their audience had sat himself up on the wood-box with his weak back supported against the corner post. At "You stranger, you oh so familiar!" the two singers lifted their hands and clasped them over their stomachs, their voices growing louder as they turned to face each other, and in the sunlight streaming through the window you could clearly see the spittle spraying from their mouths, the veins in their necks swelling up, sweat running down their foreheads, and when they sang "that sweet moment" for the second time both voices burst simultaneously into the long diminuendo.

When the singing ended there was complete silence in Andreas Lindgren's kitchen, except for the ticking of the kitchen clock. It was nearly half past one.

The listener and observer on the wood-box was sitting absolutely motionless, mouth agape and hands pressed against his collar-bones. He would never forget this, he would remember it as long as he lived. Whatever it meant.

THE PENULTIMATE HASH they were offered was mutton hash, or rather, lamb hash, in Björknäset.

The family there had held back a pot of hash in case any stranger should come by and possibly want to try it.

While Betty cooked the potatoes and set the table, her husband Edward described in detail how the much-sought-after mutton hash was made, a secret they had kept in the family ever since one of Zakarias Andersson's sons had built a house on the land more than two hundred years previously. For it was indeed a secret, a big secret incorporating a huge number of smaller secrets. He stood in the center of the floor and demonstrated with vigorous gestures how the lamb was prepared, from beginning to end.

"Even the desire for hash is inherited," he said, "ingrained in our flesh."

He swung his right arm in a great arc to illustrate how the lamb was killed with an axe, he hung the slaughtered creature by the back legs from a beam in the outhouse and put a bucket under its slit throat to collect the blood. And that was one of the secrets: the blood was cooked with the water and strained to make the stock. Then he would skin the beast as it hung, pulling away the hide with his left hand while the right wielded the knife.

For the cutting he used neither saw nor axe, but only the knife. He separated the parts of the body from one another at the points where they were originally attached, at the ligaments and cartilage and bone membrane. The offal: the liver and lungs and heart and kidneys—he held them up one after another—is stuffed into the large intestine to make sausages. Then he would cut the meat from the bone. And he smashed the bones with an axe head and let them simmer from morning to evening on the stove so that all the marrow and goodness came out into the stock. Only then was the meat itself cooked, for two hours with half a handful of sea salt, and then put through the mincer. He let them see how he turned the handle, and the mincer must have been at least four feet high. The minced meat was added to the stock and left to simmer.

He didn't need to tell them the last little secret. They could see for themselves that Betty was skinning and boning an Iceland herring, and she would add the filleted fish to the hash when it had come back to the boil so that it would melt down into the mixture. "It's the salty herring," Edward said, "that transforms the mild lamb into a good strong mutton hash."

Betty and Edward sat with them while they ate, their eyes following every mouthful from plate to gullet. Robert Maser and Lars Högström ate slowly and thoughtfully. They didn't want to break any of the rules safeguarding this ancient and traditional hash. It was dark gray and glutinous. It tasted of lamb and herring.

23

EVERY EVENING THAT summer, when he had not managed to keep an eye on their whereabouts, Bertil would come creeping up the stairs and sit himself down on a chair in one of their two rooms. He would even ask straight out, "How's it been today?" But mostly he would just sit in silence, his cap still on his head and his two sheath knives hanging against his thighs. He could probably sit like that all night long. He had boundless patience. So they told him all about it: the roads they had taken, the folk they had met, what they had seen along the way, the hash they had sampled.

And sometimes they went even further. It was hardly necessary, but one thing led to another and soon they found themselves no longer talking just to Bertil but also to each other. They sat down and produced their notebook and read out particular sentences they had written during the course of the day. They seemed to be egging each other on.

"It's fragmentation no longer capable of reconstitution,"

one of them might say. "Fibers and membranes and tissues which have found their conclusive form."

"But which at the same time," responded the second, "are totally devoid of form. Which have become pulp or pap or agglomerate, whether solid or liquid. Which can never again revert to their former state."

"And which in some cases," the first continued, "may be so tasty and irresistible that one can never be sated. One has a sense of the beginning of something new, never before experienced."

"Exactly," said the second. "With Swedish hash everything is possible. It is beyond ordered and civilized society. If life has been empty and meaningless and you encounter hash, you have to say to yourself: there is after all some foundation or core or center in the immeasurable infinity of existence. We do not have to give up."

"At the same time," the first one expanded, "you have to admit that it never allows itself to adopt any irrevocable shape or form. It is unpredictable and capricious and always seems to be hinting at something completely novel yet to come."

"Absolutely," the second continued. "It is substantial but elusive at one and the same time. The moment you think you've pinned it down it you have to admit that this particular hash is just another precursor or intimation or point of departure."

Lars Högström straightened up, jutting his head and neck forward the way he was wont to do when he sang. And Robert Maser's little eyes widened into round balls, his chubby cheeks reddened slightly, and he took his handkerchief out of his pocket to wipe away the saliva that was starting to dribble from the corners of his mouth.

"But the more you devote yourself to hash," said Lars Högström, "the deeper you get into it, the more fascinated and enthralled you become. Anyone who gets involved with hash will never be the same again. You also feel full of gratitude and want to give something in return. That's why we're making these notes."

"Yes," said Robert Maser, "we're confident enough to say that we're compiling a book on Swedish hash."

"Who would want to publish a book like that?" Bertil asked.

"Books don't need to be published," Lars Högström said. "The main thing is that they should be written."

"In these parts," said Bertil, "we've made hash since time immemorial simply because we didn't know of anything else."

24

"AS TASTERS," HE told Linda now, "they were incompetent. They had no method. No knowledge of meat or offal or cooking. They were just carried away by some kind of desire or lust."

Linda had brought him the paper so that he could read about a man who had just been discovered in Germany. He had been hiding in a cave in the Harz mountains since the end of the war, for fifty-six years. He had kept himself alive on an enormous store of freeze-dried beans and dried beef and leeks and lovage. When they got him out into the sunlight he shriveled up and died within a few hours. Some thought he was Martin Bormann, the war criminal.

"He belonged to your era, so to speak," said Linda.

"That's a newspaper article," he said. "That's all it is. It's the sort of thing they have to have in newspapers."

No, anyone who wants to be a serious taster has to rinse his mouth thoroughly, preferably with brandy, blow his nose at regular intervals and be segregated from the surrounding environment as completely as possible.

Linda remembered seeing a program on TV about food and drink tasters. They spat all the time, they filled their mouths with one thing or another and then spat it out, they kept notes on what they spat out, and they had big noses and were highly paid. The most eminent tasters came from Flanders in Holland.

"You're still hunting high and low, through field and forest?" he asked. "Looking for mountains?"

Of course. And she would do it as long as she lived.

"There's a big mountain behind Morken too," he said. "Called New mountain."

Yes, she was familiar with it.

"And beyond Lillholmträsk is Åmliden hill."

Yes, she was well aware of it. They had spoken about Åmliden several times already.

"I've scribbled and sketched out something on that paper for you," he said. "If you want it."

Yes, she did. She took the rolled-up sheet of paper that he had covered with his pictures and colors and signs, and to protect it from the rain she wrapped it in torn-out pages of the newspaper with the rediscovered German man in it.

It was to be some time before he saw Linda again.

But he went on writing, of course:

HOW COULD EVA Marklund get hold of a capercaillie?

It was Bertil who suggested it: "You could try a capercaillie!"

SO SHE GAVE him the money to buy one; he was no hunter himself. Where the capercaillie came from, from the top of which pine on Åmträsk heath, there was no knowing. It weighed thirteen pounds.

She plucked it and drew it, cut open the crop and cleaned it, because that and the heart would go in the pot too. She stripped all the meat from the legs and carefully removed the breast meat. This was early one morning. She crushed the carcass and fried it in butter with baby onions and the heart and crop, then poured water over it and put the lid on, adding a few splashes of wine vinegar at the end.

> **Capercaillie**, *Tetrao urogallus*. The largest bird of the grouse family.
> The male has glossy bluish plumage, with scarlet skin above the eyes.
> There are various sub-species, such as the Pyrenean c., the Baikal c. and the somewhat plumper Västerbothnian c.
> C. are polygamous. Hunting permitted from September till January.

She cleaned the leg meat, sliced it up and put it through the finest disk on the mincer. Meanwhile she was carefully setting a fire in the kitchen stove, one piece of wood at a time, because the capercaillie is fastidious when it comes to heat, and she minced the meat once more, with three egg yolks and one white and a pinch of salt and three white peppercorns from the pestle and mortar. That was the mixture for the meatballs.

She added a lump of homemade butter to half a glass of juniper berry juice and a drop of lingonberry juice, and stood that pan on one side to cool.

She brought in a panful of new almond potatoes from

the field and a bunch of tender young carrots from the cabbage patch. It was one o'clock now, and she sat down at the table to scrape the carrots and have a rest. Her dinner guests would be arriving in three hours. The capercaillie was going to help her drive the hash out of their heads.

The clock had struck half past two when she lifted the lid of the casserole and let the vapors from the cooking rise up towards the steam vent. She carefully added a little salt and took a few sips on a soup spoon to taste it. When about a quart of liquid was left she strained it through a muslin cloth and the colander. She poured half into a pan and mixed it with cream from Gransjö and a teaspoon of whey cheese, and that would be the sauce. She threw the carcass and crop and heart in the slop pail.

Meanwhile she was shifting the three pans and the casserole backwards and forwards over the stove all the time to find the right heat.

As the hour approached, she cut the breast meat diagonally in thin slices and laid it in a dish and poured the juniper juice and cooled butter over it, leaving it to stand and take up the flavors. The carrots and the almond potatoes, which hadn't even developed a skin, were already cooking.

Finally she took a teaspoon and lowered pellets of the meatball mixture into the casserole, which she had slid it to one side to lower the heat. The meatballs had only to set, not cook.

The plates and cutlery and glasses and the little bowl of jelly were already on the table. The napkins were freshly washed and ironed and inserted in the napkin rings.

Only when her two guests had come in and seated themselves did she complete her work on the capercaillie. She put
another four logs in the stove and moved the casserole and
the pans of carrots and potatoes to the work surface.
Whisking the still simmering sauce with her left hand, she
used her right to lift the slices of breast meat out of their
marinade and lay them directly on the top of the stove, giving them just half a minute to braise.

Then she arranged the entire capercaillie on the big yellow and green china serving dish: the breast in the center, and
in a circle around it the balls of leg meat, drizzling a few
spoonfuls of sauce over it and decorating it with a sprinkling
of lingonberries. She filled dishes of the matching set with
almond potatoes and carrots no thicker than a woman's little
finger, poured the rest of the sauce into the sauceboat and
finally set everything on the table.

"Aren't you eating with us today?" Lars Högström
asked.

"I've only made enough for two," she said. "I'm having
something different."

She sat down on the sofa, leaning forward slightly with
her eyes fixed on the meal and the diners, who began to help
themselves straightaway. They took some of everything and
mixed it together on their plates. Lars Högström even mashed
his potatoes with the sauce and the small soft meatballs. They
ate in silence, taking a sip of the juniper drink from time to
time. Lars Högström took some jelly, but Robert Maser did-
n't; one of them cut the breast meat into tiny little pieces, the
other rolled the slices and put them in his mouth whole. By

and large they seemed to be eating the capercaillie in much the same way as they ate any other food: with a dull ache of hunger, not especially intense but nevertheless insatiable.

Bertil had now taken up his usual position on the chair by the door, and he too was observing them.

When the meat dish and the carrots and the sauce boat and even the bowl of jelly were empty, Lars Högström said, "That wasn't at all bad. What was it you said this meal was called?"

"It was capercaillie," Bertil replied, straightening his cap.

"You must do that again," said Lars Högström.

"If you can't think of anything else," said Robert Maser.

BY THE TIME the writer had got this far, to the eating of the capercaillie, fifty-three years later, to be exact, the Council Leader finally received a reply from the head of the publishing house in Stockholm. It was quite brief, and the signature illegible. Having read it, he immediately took it to his secretary to show her. "This," he said, "is how Stockholm behaves towards Västerbotten. This is how Stockholmers have always written to Västerbothnians."

The publisher expressed his thanks for the letter and the offer. Publishing was a difficult and often loss-making enterprise, subject to the laws and demands of the market. The sort of material that justified the cost of printing was that which had broad appeal to the reading public. Right now there was a demand for books by very young authors with diverse and unusual experience of life in the big cities. They already had writers of advanced years on their list, even from Norrland, and as the person responsible for their publishing program he had had enough, more than enough, of the ineffective and unfruitful, at times even nihilistic, writing of old age. In conclusion, he would suggest that the Council itself take on the printing of the work of this obviously manically productive old man. There might well be a subsidy available from the EU in Brussels that would offset some of their losses.

"IT'S TERRIBLE HAVING to bear the responsibility for all this," said the Councilor.

But his secretary consoled him: "He'll be dead soon, anyway."

25

NOW THE ONLY one remaining was Ellen in Lillsjöliden. That was also what Eva Marklund said to Lars Högström, as he lay at her side. The day had come to its end, the day she had cooked capercaillie in vain. "Now all that remains is the hash in Lillsjöliden," she said, "Ellen's hash." There was a sigh of resignation in her voice.

Yes, he said. According to his notes it would be their twenty-fourth trip. They had been putting it off. But go they must. He knew they should have gone to Lillsjöliden long before, that in fact the most sensible thing might have been to go to Ellen in Lillsjöliden at the very beginning.

They had said it to one another often enough. And everywhere they had gone people had pointed it out to them. That there was hash in Lillsjöliden which was the model, in a sense, for all other hash; which particularly in aftertaste was perfection itself. Extremely few had tried it: it was known mainly by repute. No, in this house, in this village, at this table, there was nobody who had actually ever eaten it.

All that summer he and Robert Maser had been postponing Lillsjöliden for the future, perhaps because they felt a slight apprehension, perhaps because other trips would seem meaningless after the peerless hash in Lillsjöliden, or perhaps because they thought they might experience such an anticlimax that it would sap their energy and desire. And they had also wanted to keep something first-class and sublime to look forward to. Since it had to be conceded: they had also tasted failures.

But now it could be put off no longer. Fall had arrived, and the special motorcycle gear that Robert Maser had taken from his stock had started cracking and splitting. And the suspicion was dawning on him that their travels and researches had become too well known and talked about, that some households were preparing food especially for his and Robert Maser's sake, food that was titivated with strange spices and sweetening and coloring agents, that some housewives were treating them, with the best intentions, to pure and simple fakes.

"And there'll be another summer next year," he said.

He had got into the habit of letting his left hand play with her necklace of white china beads when he was lying next to her. And she rubbed her cheek against his shoulder while ruffling the hair below his navel with her right hand. They had both sweated a little but had quickly dried off again.

"The really genuine," Eva said, "is so woefully rare. If it even occurs at all."

"I'd never thought about it," he said. "But that may well be true."

"And what sort of people are you?" said Ellen in Lillsjöliden. "To come here and frighten the chickens? And the poor rabbits!"

"We're sorry," said Lars Högström. "It's our motorbike. It makes a bit of a noise. It's called a Diamond."

She had just come out of the cattle shed and had two tin buckets in her hand. Her black rubber boots had been mended with red patches, her apron was stiff and gray with dirt and remnants of food, and she had a ragged shawl across her shoulders. Her body was lopsided, as they knew: it had been mentioned to them beforehand. Many years ago she had got caught in the peat digger and one breast had been sliced off and several ribs crushed. But she had survived.

She obviously wanted them to know how unexpected their visit was. "I've got such an awful lot to do," she said. "I haven't really got any time for strangers."

Her face was disfigured with scrofula. Her eyes were red and suppurating, the corners of her mouth ulcerated and her lips swollen and shapeless. Her left eyelid sagged loosely half way down over her eye. Her cheeks and forehead and chin were red with eczema and small fistulas.

"I can't believe that you gentlemen have business here," she said, moving off towards the house. "Business with me?"

She had a strangely shuffling and swaying gait, as if her feet were continually getting stuck in the uncut grass. As they followed her Robert Maser whispered to Lars Högström, "I can't bring myself to look at her!"

"You haven't looked properly!" Lars Högström whispered back. "Have a good look and you'll soon get used to her!"

In the kitchen she stood the buckets on the table. Her two uninvited guests shifted a couple of cardboard cartons full of chicken feathers and sat down on the lid of the kitchen bench, which was covered with a shabby, torn quilt. The stench indoors was indescribable sour, sweet and oppressive. After only a few minutes Robert Maser had to run out and spew behind the rhubarb bed. But he came back.

"I'm letting the pig swill ferment," Ellen said, "it's easier to mix. But it smells a bit."

> **Scrofula** (*Scrophulae*). The symptoms of s. manifest themselves in a series of inflammatory processes on the skin and mucous membranes, particularly on the lips, nose and eyes.
>
> The more advanced the disease, the more common the incidence of tuberculosis of the glands or bones.
>
> S. is particularly prevalent among the poorer classes.
>
> In the early stages a prognosis may be favorable, but the outcome of the disease is generally fatal.

THEN SHE REVERTED to her question: no one would travel around these desolate regions on such a remarkable motorbike that might explode at any time on Västerbotten's appalling roads without having some definite business, would they?

She spoke mostly out of the left corner of her mouth. The right was immobile under its scrofulous skin.

"We just wanted to call on you," said Lars Högström. "We're calling on everyone."

"We'd heard about you," said Robert Maser. "Lots of people have spoken about you."

"And about your cooking," Lars Högström added.

"Your cooking is renowned far and wide," said Robert Maser.

"I only cook one sort of food," said Ellen. "But on the other hand it's very versatile."

"Oh," said Lars Högström. "And what sort of food might it be?"

"It's hash," said Ellen.

"Exactly," said Robert Maser, nodding to Lars Högström. "Exactly the dish that everyone's been mentioning."

"That's right," said Lars Högström. "Hash. That was it."

She pulled out a stool from under the table and sat down.

"Well, there's nothing special about it," she said. "I could let you try some. But I'm tubercular. There might be infection in the hash."

"We're immune," said Robert Maser.

"We're completely unsusceptible," said Lars Högström. "Did you say it was hash that the dish was called?"

"Yes, hash."

"I think I'm correct in saying," Lars Högström continued, "that this hash of yours is the most famous dish in upcountry Västerbotten."

"It's known even down on the coast," Robert Maser confirmed.

"To me it's just ordinary," said Ellen. "But I've heard that folk talk about it."

"That's an understatement," said Robert Maser.

"I can't see why," said Ellen. "But there's been a steady stream of people coming here and wanting to taste it. And I've been tubercular for twenty years. So I can only repeat: there's bound to be infection in the hash."

"It's only right," said Lars Högström. "It's what love of thy neighbor expects of us."

"There are pretty certain to be tubercles in the hash, is what I usually tell them," she went on. "I let them choose between life and hash. And they choose life. But after a while they regret it and wish they'd opted for hash instead."

While she was talking she was scratching her cheeks from time to time with both hands. She wasn't actually coughing, but every now and again she had to spit into one of the slop pails.

"That's why there's a lot of talk about this hash," she said. "If it's famous, that's the reason."

"We don't need to choose," said Robert Maser. "We're immune. We can go for both the hash and life."

"I see," she said. "Well, in that case."

SHE TOOK TWO plates from the rack and disappeared outside to the cold-store. Lars Högström and Robert Maser used the time to make space at the table, putting the tin buckets down on the floor, folding up the old newspapers and sweeping the breadcrumbs and potato peelings and plum stones into a little pile that Robert Maser carried out and threw onto the grass. By the time Ellen returned they were ready.

It was the darkest hash they had ever seen. And as soon as she came in the door all the old musty smell was displaced, leaving only the ripe aroma of spices and meat and offal, heavy and pregnant with significance but at the same time titillating and uplifting. She set the plates in front of them and they said nothing, not even a word of thanks, they just sat quietly inhaling the hash, which seemed to be giving off steam despite being cold. Ellen, who had sat down on the stool again, noticed that they were not even daring to look at each other. They leaned forward till their noses were almost touching the hash, and they breathed so deep that their motorcycle jackets creaked and crackled. They closed their eyes for minutes at a time. The only other sound was Ellen's hawking.

"This is last year's hash," she said. "But that doesn't mean anything. It's always the same all the years I've been making it."

When they finally started eating they used no implements. They broke off small fragments with their fingers and pressed them against the roof of their mouths, where the hash dissolved of its own accord and trickled over their tongues and molars. They didn't chew, they let the air filter in between their lips so that nothing of the experience would be lost, and they delayed swallowing as long as they could.

Ellen's hash seemed not to contain individual constituents, they could discern no graininess and no corn or fiber, it was a harmonious blend of unknown ingredients, molded into a whole and sufficient unto themselves. There was no reason to ask any questions about this hash, nor to make any notes. They imbibed it, they let themselves be permeated by it, in silence and in solemn gratitude.

Nevertheless Robert Maser eventually broke the silence. They had been eating for over an hour despite the fact that the pieces she had put before them were no bigger than the palm of the hand. He said, "One can only wonder what hash like this can be made of."

"Just about everything goes into it," Ellen said simply.

"I MUST MAKE sure the bike is still there," said Lars Högström eventually. And he got up and went out. Robert Maser stayed where he was. He was looking at Ellen now, he observed her minutely, her face and her lopsided body. He even smiled at her, with warmth and affection. When she too stood up and went out he was alone in the kitchen. The clock on the wall above his head had stopped on half past six and the last flies of summer were buzzing around him.

Ellen found Lars Högström by the corner of the cattle shed, leaning back against the timbers. When she put her hand on the cracked arm of his motorcycle jacket she could feel him trembling.

"Was it too strong?" she asked. "Was it too much for you?"

"It's nothing," he said. "I can take anything. It might be a touch of emotion. I never thought anything like that could exist."

"I've been waiting for you two," she said. "I've been waiting all summer. In the end I didn't think you'd be coming at all."

"We kept putting it off," he said. "We knew this would

be something beyond the norm. We didn't have the courage. Our expectations held us back."

"But I don't want you to sing for me," she said. "I'm not that type."

There hadn't yet been a frost, so they were having to strike at mosquitoes all the time as they were talking. Her hand was still resting on his arm.

"When are you cooking next?" he asked.

"St. Simon's Day," she said. "The twenty-eighth of October. Always on St. Simon's Day. That's in three days' time."

26

LINDA USED TO cut his hair, which was growing ever thicker and darker.

"She'll be back soon," the other staff said when he asked after her.

"She never mentioned that she was going to abandon me," he said. "She might have got lost. You can never rely on maps. There's a precipice above Inreliden that you can't see and you could easily fall headlong over it. And the bog at Oxkall spring is bottomless. Anyone could disappear there."

"She's only on leave," they reminded him. "She's coming back."

"Not to mention illness," he went on. "There are illnesses you've never heard of. Dysentery and catarrh and stroke and dropsy and plague and pox and cholera and as many others as you like to name."

"Linda is healthier and stronger than any of us."

"Everyone is susceptible to everything," he said. "No one can ever be certain. And Linda is a more sensitive person than you might think."

"As soon as she gets back," they said, "we'll send her to you."

"Susceptibility," he said, "is an illness in itself. If it weren't for susceptibility, it would be a joy to be alive."

It was Niklas who took over his hairdressing. First he cropped his hair with scissors as close as he could, and then he used a powerful shaver to reveal the bare skin, which turned out to be shiny and healthy and unblemished. The former newspaper correspondent ran both hands over his head. "Does it really have to be like this?" he asked.

"Yes," said Niklas, "that's how it's going to be from now on."

And from then on his head was shaved every week.

LARS HÖGSTRÖM WASN'T coming downstairs any more in the evenings to sleep at Eva Marklund's side. He didn't even say, "I won't be coming tonight." He just didn't turn up.

It might have had something to do with the summer holidays being over. He always had schoolwork to correct. And he and Robert Maser had received a book of Franz Liszt songs in the mail. Singing also took up time. The school had acquired a new harmonium; the old one, which was a bit leaky, had been carried up to Robert Maser's room, and he often sat practicing with the Hymnal open in front of him. The red and yellow leaves of the aspen trees and birches were fluttering in the breeze, the potato haulms had been burnt by the frost, and mist and damp were rising over Avabäck Stream.

"Are you depressed by the fall?" Eva asked.

No, not in the least. For him the fall was the season for new plans and broader horizons and contemplation of icy times to come. His life had always been an autumnal life, even his childhood had been autumnal in a way. "You can think so clearly in the fall," he said. "You're uplifted." He might still be singing simple songs from time to time, but his feelings as the fall arrived were principally symphonic.

"But you're not coming to me at night any more?" Eva eventually plucked up the courage to say.

"A schoolteacher," said Bertil, who of course had been sitting listening without their noticing, "a schoolteacher always has his sights on higher and more refined things. So why should he creep down the stairs at night?"

When the time drew near, Lars Högström announced a fall vacation for the school in Avabäck. The pupils could do with a few days' rest before the onset of winter. He did it with reference to school regulations, to special circumstances, which certainly prevailed up in the north. The children would be able to help with carrying in the wood, for instance, during these days off, but otherwise they should put their feet up against the wall timbers that were now warming up and learn the pages in their textbooks that he would assign. The name Kvarken denotes the two broadest channels in the northern

Baltic. A number divided by itself gives a quotient of one. Passion is spelled with double s.

He told Eva Marklund and Robert Maser that he was going down to Ångermanland on his own, to see his home village before the snows came and before he had to put a cover and blankets over the Diamond for the winter. He didn't know where he would be staying, but in that sparsely populated region around Dorotea and Hoting and Brännberget you were welcome at any house you came to, when there were any houses at all. "I always get by," he said. And he had a near relative in Dorotea, an uncle.

ON THURSDAY 28TH October, early in the morning, he mounted his motorcycle and set off. "You ought to wear something warmer and more waterproof," Eva had said. "I'd like you back healthy and in one piece, after all."

And she had pointed out the cracks and leaks in his clothing.

> **Dorotea**. Village on the inland railroad. Ca 2000 inh. D. is situated on a hill north of the Bergvatten River and close to Bergvatten Lake.
>
> In 1941 the poet Gunnar Ekelöf participated in the National March in D. and wrote the major portion of his *Ferry Song* in Byström's Guest House.

"Nothing will happen to me," he said. "I can't even catch a cold. And anyway, I'm heading south."

It was going to be empty at Eva's table, because Robert Maser was also preparing for departure. His stocks were still not exhausted, and there were crofts and smallholdings around Vilhelmina and Latikberg or Knaften and Hornmyr that he had not yet visited. Eva had made sandwiches of oven-dried lamb for him and given him a bag of turnips from the cabbage patch. As he climbed in and was about to close the door of the bus, he heard Bertil's voice behind him.

"So you think the schoolteacher is really going to Ångermanland?"

"Of course," Robert Maser replied. "That motorbike is as reliable as a Swiss watch. He'll get to Ångermanland all right."

"Oh, sure," said Bertil, "a motorbike can always be relied on."

Robert Maser stood inside the open bus door. "I've been hundreds of miles on that bike, behind Lars Högström. With my hands on his shoulders or clasped round his chest, I've felt more secure than ever before in my life."

"In an hour or two," said Bertil, "there'll be a cloud spreading over the whole district and there'll be wonderful appetizing aromas wafting everywhere and people will realize what day it is today. But by then you'll already be in Husbondliden or Lycksele."

"I may take the route through Björksele and Kattisavan," Robert Maser replied.

"Though Lars Högström," Bertil continued, "he'll be in the right place, the only right place, and he won't miss a thing."

"Ångermanland?" said Robert Maser. "Is Ångermanland the only right place to be?"

"You've never understood Lars Högström," said Bertil. "You've never seen through him. He's the kind of person who needs to be seen through."

"He's the only friend I've got in the world; as far as I remember, the only friend I've ever had," Robert Maser said. "And he's immune. Why should I make any effort to see through him?"

Bertil could no longer content himself with veiled hints and innuendos: "He's a deceiver," he said. "He may not even be the man he makes himself out to be. He pretends to read the music at the harmonium, but in reality he's playing by ear. He's been whoring with Eva and now he's deserted her. And in the book he's writing about hash your name isn't even mentioned."

"Is that really true?"

"I've read every word myself," said Bertil.

No, Lars Högström hadn't gone to Ångermanland! And what was Ångermanland anyway? The truth was that Lars Högström was to be found much closer to home.

"Those," said Robert Maser, "are very serious accusations. And he's usually the one who reads the music when we sing."

"Anyone who wants to know the truth," said Bertil, "can drive over and see with his own eyes. And I would never sing to his tune myself."

"Well, I can allow myself a little detour," said Robert Maser. "Your lies and insinuations can't be left unchallenged."

So he drove his bus westwards instead of south. At Lillsjön he parked on the empty timber ground at the edge of Kalviken bay, and walked up the hill through the forest. The oldest trees had been felled the previous winter and he had to push rough branches and discarded foliage aside to get through.

Above the abandoned gravel pit he found a few clumps of bright frostbitten blueberries and paused for a while to pick and eat some.

When he reached the mounds of stones at the edge of the field, by the barbed-wire fence, he stopped. From there he had a view of the whole of Lillsjöliden. The house and the underground cold-store in the hillside and the cattle shed and the barn and the farmyard, and the smoke rising vertically through the light, serene, slightly greenish-tinged shimmering air.

27

The big cauldron was on the fire outside near the cold-store, half full of water, and there was a pile of birch logs beside it. The fire was already lit when he arrived. Ellen didn't look up at him, her gaze was fixed on the crows flocking over Lillsjöliden.

"You can put that machine in the barn doorway!" she shouted. "And bring the axe that's in the doorpost!"

The axe had a small shaft but was hand forged and heavy. He had to carry it in both hands; he was not used to axes.

"You can split this," she said, dropping at his feet the reindeer head she had brought out of the cold-store. "It was a reindeer cow," she said, "there's nothing better."

The water in the cauldron was coming up to the boil, with peppercorns and cloves and bay leaves floating on the surface. "The hooves are already in," she said. "The reindeer hooves." And as she threw in a handful of the little yellow onions, she said, "That's the onions."

She carried on the same way, involving him with a running commentary on the whole recipe. "That's . . ." she told him as she threw one ingredient after another into the boiling broth.

Before he could split the skull he had to flay it. Despite the fact that the knife Ellen gave him had a long blade and was newly sharpened, and despite her showing him where to make the first incisions, he found it very hard for his delicate teacher fingers. He had to use both hands and cut away flap by flap.

When it was finally skinned and split she brought over a bucket of water and he scooped out the shattered brain and rinsed the skull before adding it solemnly to the pot.

Ellen had spread a sheepskin on the grass, still wet from the frost, and they sat down. She had also brought out a pan of cold coffee and a few pieces of flatbread. Seeing her now for the first time eating and drinking, he noticed how surprisingly strong and white her teeth were. She got up periodically to fetch something from the cold-store and add it to what was already cooking. She seemed to have everything and anything down there in the cold-store.

"That's the pigs' heads," she said.

And, "That's the calf chine."

And then, "That's the cow muzzle and the calf's heart."

He too stood up once or twice to put some more wood on the fire. But he made no notes, he didn't even have his notebook and pen with him. That was not the reason he was there.

"That's the goat's cheese," she had occasion to say a little later.

AT LUNCHTIME SHE fetched a plate of cold boiled potatoes and the last but one basin of the previous year's hash. They looked at each other as they ate, smiling and confident, and they let their fingers touch when they took more helpings from the plate or the basin. But she didn't forget the task they were engaged on.

"That's the flanks and the midriff."

"That's the tongues."

He leaned back, supporting himself on his elbow, now and then licking the fingers of his free right hand. She sat with her arms around her drawn-up knees, her remaining breast pressing against the top of her thigh, and dried her rheumy eyes with the sleeve of her sweater. The implement she was using to stir the pot was a ten-pronged pitchfork. "It mustn't catch," she said. "If it burns we have to start all over again from the beginning, because it'll go like tar."

"But why," he ventured to ask as he poked at the logs with a fence post he had found by the sheep shed, "why can't you put all the ingredients in the pot first and then add the requisite amount of water and let the whole lot cook for as many days as it needs?"

No, that would be unthinkable, no one would be so stupid, it would be a transgression against all she had been taught. To everything there is a season. A time for liver, and a time for heart, a time for salt and a time for cooking carrots and taking them out, a time to add water and a time for pouring off excess water.

And sure enough she fished out some carrots with the

pitchfork and threw them on the grass, then ladled out a few drops of the liquid.

"If the fact is," she said, "that you don't believe in my cooking, if you're uncertain about my hash, then you'd better go to Inreliden or Brännberg or Lauparliden or anywhere else your motorcycle might take you!"

At this he ran up to her and seized both her hands in his and assured her that he believed implicitly, he was prepared to sacrifice anything for her and her hash, he had just been feeling so comfortable on the sheepskin that he had allowed his thoughts to wander in erroneous directions.

And a few minutes later she went to fetch some white enameled tin mugs of spices that were still needed and emptied them into the pot.

"That's ginger.

"That's strong pepper.

"That's currant leaves.

"That's molasses."

HAVING RETURNED TO his bus to get his bag of food, Robert Maser was now sitting on a flat stone at the edge of the line of boulders by the barbed wire fence. He had split one of the turnips down the middle and was scraping it out with a spoon, slowly and methodically. Lillsjöliden lay before and above him with its little storehouses and barns and its cultivated plots and cabbage patches and potato beds, and the house itself. He could also see the cold-store and the fire and the cauldron and the two hash cooks out in front, the two working colleagues busy with wood and pitchfork and fence post and ingredients. They were in no hurry, they were moving around calmly and tranquilly, apparently conversing at intervals. They were completely on their own over there in Lillsjöliden, and the fumes and vapors from the cauldron were so thick and heavy that the sky was obscured, and they themselves were enveloped in the steam and the almost oppressive smells.

A little further down the hillside Bertil lay behind a sallow bush. He could see Robert Maser very clearly. And he could see that Robert Maser could see something: his head was turning slightly every now and again, he would shade his eyes from the sun with his hand, once or twice raising his arm to point as if he couldn't quite believe what he was seeing or as if he wanted to imprint it on his memory. But Bertil couldn't see what Robert Maser saw, he could only observe the observer. Had he tried to crawl forward he would have revealed his presence.

Robert Maser stayed where he was on his stone. It was late afternoon and the two figures cooking and tending the fire by the cold-store were still going about their tasks, occasionally disappearing into the house, but it was impossible to tell what they were doing inside. Towards twilight Lars Högström took the sheepskin indoors, and the gaps between visible activities by the fire lengthened. Before the evening light completely faded, Ellen emerged to put something in the pot. He could just make out her misshapen lips in motion but couldn't hear what she was saying:

"That's the pig's liver."

BUT BERTIL MADE his way home to Avabäck in the semi-darkness, if home was the right concept in his case, and he told Eva Marklund that neither of her lodgers would be coming back that night; in fact it wasn't certain that they would ever return.

"I knew that," Eva said. "Lars is in Ångermanland, maybe staying in Dorotea, and Robert Maser is up in Vilhelmina."

So Bertil felt compelled to explain the truth of the matter to her. Everyone would have known that hash was being made today in Lillsjöliden, it was no secret. And down by the barbed wire fence of the lowest field the clothier was sitting on a flat stone keeping a watchful eye on the process. And up on the far side of the hill, beside the cold-store, very close, indeed shamefully close, to Ellen of Lillsjöliden, was Lars Högström. That at least was his conviction. He had only been able to see the one who was actually doing the seeing, but he was used to drawing conclusions. He was not easily fooled. He was not one to let himself be deceived.

"Well," said Eva, "that was what I'd half suspected in my heart of hearts. Would you like some oatmeal?"

As he ate his oatmeal he carried on talking to her.

What had happened was almost unbearable. He had never experienced the like before. To have to make do with just the reflection of immediate events, not to be able to see for himself, to have to content himself with the gestures of the viewer! And not being able to hear anything! Worst of all was the lack of uniformity and balance, the unholy segregation of participants and observers and the despised and rejected witnesses and spectators, in fact all that he had now seen through: the sin against the self-evident.

"If you like," said Eva, "I can heat up the rest of the oatmeal in the morning."

"Oh, yes please," said Bertil. "With lingonberries and butter."

ROBERT MASER WAS still sitting on the flat stone at the edge of the pile. The scents from the simmering cauldron came drifting across the hillside towards the lake. It was nearly dark now, and not much could be seen of the two figures watching and tending the cooking. There were sounds of one of them coming out and stirring the cauldron with the pitchfork and putting some logs on the embers, and when the flames leapt up he could even discern which of them it was. There was a faint light in the kitchen window, and a few sparks and smoke to be seen from the chimney. Ellen's goats beyond the potato field were no longer bleating.

In the last few hours before dawn the grass and heaps of stones and Robert Maser were covered in frost. He was resting his head in his hands, and for brief moments he almost managed to sleep.

At sunrise his eyes sharpened into focus, he sat up and rubbed his nose and cheeks with the palms of his hands, straightened his shoulders and resumed his watch. When Ellen came out and fetched something from the cold-store and put it in the steaming liquid he could even just about make out her words: "That's the goat's lungs."

"ON THE SECOND day," said Ellen, "everything just has to be kept going. It has to be simmering and bubbling, over embers not flames, and you have to keep stirring it with the pitchfork, but hardly anything should be added."

Lars Högström, who had slept on the kitchen floor with only the sheepskin beneath him, was rubbing at the stiffness in his muscles and joints before hungrily repeating, "Hardly anything?"

So she gave him the task of adding the penultimate item, pine resin. He went across to the edge of the forest and pulled a lump of resin directly off the bark, and when he dropped it in the pot, he said, "That's the pine resin."

The final ingredient was gall, and she fetched that out of the cold-store. It was the gall-bladder of the reindeer, and she squeezed out the only possible and appropriate number of drops.

Down the hill everything was as it had been the day before: an observer observing the observed and another observer observing the observer. "This could take some time," Eva had said as she stuffed a bag of sliced blood sausage into Bertil's pocket.

The heat under the cauldron was no longer what it had been, but the intensity of the aromatic fumes and vapors had not diminished. Eva herself stood for a moment alone on her steps in Avabäck and sniffed the breeze from the northwest.

> **Swedish hash**, *pölsa* (dial. *pylsa* or *palscha*). Dish comprising finely ground meat, usually offal, in its own jelly. Minced meat. Originally *bulscha*, from the Greek *balsamon*, deriving from a Semitic word denoting a viscous mixture of resin and fragrant volatile oils (see Balsam spruce), thence balsamic. Figuratively: consolation, mercy, healing or alleviation.

Lars Högström carried out the two spindleback chairs that still had any spindles left for them to sit in comfort in front of the cauldron and the fire. "I've never had such an elegant and dignified hash-making session before," Ellen said.

As they stirred the pot now, pieces of bone and half skulls and gristle stuck in the prongs of the fork, bleached white and drained of all nourishment, and were thrown out onto the grass.

Then they consumed the very last of the hash in the last of the basins from the previous year. He pulled the chairs closer to the fire and the cauldron so that the aromas from the present cooking floated over basin and plates like a sauce. He had placed the chairs so close together that their hands and fingers hardly needed to distinguish one mouth from the other.

"I think there's a meaning to everything after all," he said between bites.

"I've never thought about it," she said.

The contents of the hash now seemed to be more fermenting than cooking, big blue shimmering bubbles covered the surface, the color was deepening and the rising vapors were changing from a whitish-gray to brown and dark green.

They would be able to sample it by the evening of the second day.

AS THE HEAT and acridity and taste of medicine or possibly alcohol seeped into him, he said, "Has anyone ever told you how beautiful you are?"

"Probably no one ever thought to say it," she replied. "They've all just been after the hash."

Down the hill, behind the straggling sallow bush, lay Bertil. He could see Robert Maser now occasionally shaking his head, sometimes almost standing up but then sinking back down onto his stone, and even raising his arms and clenching his fists at the sky. He also saw him setting to work on the last turnip, probably saving his sandwiches for later.

That evening Bertil told Eva he really couldn't endure it any longer, not a day more. Robert Maser might well stay sitting on his stone and blocking his path indefinitely.

"I've been thinking a lot," he said to Eva.

"You always do," she replied.

His insides were being gnawed away, he said. An emptiness had been hollowed out inside him. Or rather a bubble or blister full of turbulent and highly explosive emotions. The shame of not being the one who was actually seeing, of having to watch and perceive only at second hand, of being an interpreter instead of an observer he could no longer bear the ignominy of it, not for another whole day.

"You'd better do something about it, then," said Eva.

THAT NIGHT, THE second, Lars Högström slept not on the floor but by Ellen's side on the wadding mattress on the convertible sofa. He got up three times, quietly and carefully so as not to wake her, and went and put more logs on the fire.

The very next night he would say, "I'll lie on the outside,

you take the thick pillow and I'll have the flat one. The quilt will easily cover both of us, we'll do as we've always done, we'll lie as we've always lain. Since time immemorial."

28

ON THE THIRD day it should never burn, but just glow. Ellen sent him over to the birch grove behind the cattle shed with a bow saw and axe to cut up some green logs that would only hiss and smolder. The liquid was thickening in the pot, the steam was turning thin and transparent, there was nothing sticking to the prongs of the fork any more. They took frequent greedy gulps from their ladle, blowing on it to cool it down.

When the hoarfrost on the largely immobile Robert Maser had turned to dew, he sat up and bolted down his sandwiches. The morning mist which had covered Lillsjöliden for an hour or so drifted away and the two hash cooks were clearly visible, at times even bathed in sunlight. The lamb in his sandwiches was salty and tender.

Bertil had returned to his same position after all. But he no longer lay loosely coiled behind the leafless sallow bush, no, he was poised on his hands and knees, leaning forward like a runner on the starting block. He had slept behind the stove in the schoolroom, and in the morning Eva had given him buttermilk and some cheese to dip in his coffee.

Whenever Ellen and Lars Högström disappeared into the house now, they covered the cauldron with a huge wooden lid so that birds wouldn't drown in the hash.

Robert Maser could see it. But Bertil couldn't.

If anyone had been lying further down the hillside keeping an eye on Bertil, he would have noticed Bertil sometimes shifting his weight to his hands and lifting his head as if searching for something above and beyond Robert Maser, his whole body trembling.

And in the end he really did set off, with the most amazingly fast sprint up the hill, his feet stirring up the dead leaves and twigs from the previous year's felling, kicking large clumps of reindeer lichen and bog moss off stones and bedrock. Robert Maser had just seen the two Lillsjöliden cooks come out and lift the lid of the hash and slowly and intently carry out yet another tasting before going back into the house. Lars Högström had his right arm round Ellen's lopsided shoulders.

Bertil came hurtling up, skidded to an abrupt halt, turned, teetering slightly on his numb legs, and could not bring himself to speak. It was now almost three o'clock. He had drawn his two knives from their sheaths and was holding them up in front of him, both at exactly the same height. Then he started hacking and stabbing with one knife from the right and the other from the left, with absolute simultaneity. They sank deep into Robert Maser's somewhat spongy body.

He made no attempt at self-defense, holding himself upright for some time, even managing to speak a few words. Bertil paused momentarily, the knives briefly at thigh level and the corners of his mouth both turned down at precisely the same second in rigid equilateral astonishment. But then he set the knives in motion again. Robert Maser's final utterance was: "Has justice caught up with me at last?" To which Bertil panted in reply: "What justice?"

As HE FINISHED writing that last word, justice, in Sunnybank Rest Home, and inscribing his graceful and beautifully curved question mark, there came a knock at his door. It was Niklas. He had brought a letter. He closed his notebook and tucked the pen down the spiral binder. He sat on the bed to inspect the envelope. His name was typewritten, and someone had written under it in red ink BY HAND. He opened it with his unused plastic butter knife. It was from the Leader of the Council.

HE WAS CONCERNED, the Councilor wrote, extremely concerned. These were hard times, and it was a difficult and heavy burden he had to bear on behalf of the Borough Council. The ratio between consumers and producers was deteriorating, the tax base was shrinking, economies and retrenchments were inevitable. He himself had had to cut back on various things over the last few lean years. In the present situation all budget heads, all activities and all care home residents had to be put under the microscope, so to speak.

As far as the recipient of this letter was concerned, the Council had been keeping itself apprised of the situation for some time. They knew he wrote. The Council had no objection to residents writing; on the contrary, they had even organized writing courses. But the writing to which the addressee devoted himself was not like other people's, it went to extremes, it appeared to have no end, and above all it was wasteful of resources. The Council itself had explored the possibilities of rendering his writing income generating in some way, but without success. The cost of materials in his case thus had to be allocated to the normal care budget. The Council had already realized the asset of his modest home, and his state pension was inadequate, especially since he was allowed to retain pocket money, which, they were reliably informed, he used for the purchase of brandy.

A further factor had now come to light. The Council's attorney had advised them that his writing should be regarded as being in the service of the Council, that the growing collections of spiral-bound notebooks were in effect public documents. The whole affair might be taken up by the local newspaper.

"And moreover," the Councilor continued, "some of the people you write about are still alive."

To sum up, he, as Leader of the Council, was obliged to take action of some kind, to make a decision.

This letter was thus intended to convey, as considerately and sympathetically as possible, the nature of that decision.

His writing must cease forthwith. He should regard his work as concluded. The Council was obliged, in the light of the above, to prohibit him from all further writing activity. With all good wishes, Yours sincerely, etc.

WHEN NIKLAS BROUGHT him his evening meal, he told him to take the writing-stand and the pile of notebooks away. "Put them in the cellar or the attic or the pantry," he said. "If there's such a thing as a pantry in this place."

And that very same evening he began to compose in his mind the reply he would send. He thanked the Councilor for his letter. It meant for him of course a reversion to a previous, now almost forgotten, prohibition, but also restoration and liberation. In this new yet familiar situation he would like to bring the following to the Council's attention:

29

WHAT WOULD BERTIL do with Robert Maser's body?

That would have to remain a question for the Council, since they had assumed responsibility for the unwritten. He saw no reason to offer his assistance on the matter.

But as for Lars Högström, the schoolteacher, he would like to advise the Council that on the evening of the third day, prior to his aforementioned retiring for the night, the latter had become aware of an irritating burning and itching on his face and a dull but perceptible soreness in his lower airways. Ellen put her scrofulous lips to his forehead and said, "It feels like a fever. But you can't be sick?"

"Certainly not!" he replied. "I can never fall sick again! It might be the hash that's made me hot. I'm immune."

"But it's exactly the same hash as yesterday," she said. "And you had no problems with that."

"I've become so involved with this hash," he said, "that I've become part of it. I've absorbed it in a different way."

What befell Lars Högström over the next few months is predictable enough and need not be committed to writing.

On the other hand, the Council ought to put on record the fact that Manfred Marklund came home to Eva. It was spring again, and Eva had been digging furrows in the potato field. There was no one to pull the potato plough, which was why she was digging. The potatoes on the bench in the cattle shed window already had long tubers. She was standing at the sink chopping carrots, preparing dinner for the new schoolteacher. He didn't eat meat, only vegetables, and was just a temporary replacement. She had no idea Manfred was coming. He knocked on the door before walking in, which was what they had learned to do at the sanitarium in Hällnäs. She was forced to sit down for a few moments on the kitchen chair beneath the wall clock. He had arrived on the Malå bus. He was carrying his suitcase in his hand and wearing a gray striped suit and even a tie. His face was much fuller and smoother than before, and his jacket wasn't quite big enough across his chest and stomach. Their initial conversation was somewhat confused and difficult to put in writing. Though nothing is beyond the Council.

"Oh, please sit down," Eva said.

"Thanks, very kind of you," he replied, lowering himself onto the kitchen bench.

"Are you doing potatoes?" he asked.

"Yes," she replied.

The kitchen clock began to strike so they sat and listened to the four strokes. Then she stood up and put the potatoes on the stove.

"It's unbelievable how well you look," she said.

"I'm completely cured," he said. "I've been given a clean bill of health."

To which he added, "In fact I'm more than well. I'm immune."

"Glory be to God!" said Eva. "I've prayed for you every night."

"Every single night?"

"More or less."

"I see someone's started building on Matilda Holmström's land," he said. "I noticed it from the bus. There was wooden scaffolding up."

"It's the insurance company," Eva said. "People should-n't build on that site."

"And the birds have the migrants started arriving yet?"

"Yes, the cranes are here."

"It's a bit frightening and over-stimulating to be sudden-ly restored to health," he said. "Like being risen from the dead."

"Of course it is."

"We'll keep the forest," he said. "Even if I can't wield an axe or a saw any more. And you can keep the animal in the cow shed if you want. And we can rent out the hay meadow."

"So nothing will be the same as before?" she said.

"When you've become immune," he said, "you know there's no going back. No. What should start now is a new life, our new life. It's only fools who believe that things can be repeated, and they know nothing about cause and effect."

As he said this he went up to her and laid his arm across her shoulder blade. He clenched his fist and let his knuckles run slowly down her spine as if he were counting the vertebrae. Eva managed a smile at last. It was like a special code; that was the very first thing he had done to her body once a long time ago.

Then he sat down on the bench again and explained everything to her. As she must already have realized, he was a changed man. He was no longer a manual worker or lumberjack or even a farmer. He had acquired a certain amount of education and become a man of learning. Anyone who reads his way through an entire library would turn out like that. And this last month in the sanitarium, when he had begun to understand where all this was leading, he had spent his time making preparations for his discharge. Everything was planned and settled, he even had typewritten signed contracts in his case with figures and precisely formulated conditions of employment.

"But what is it you're going to do?" Eva asked.

"I'm going to write articles for the newspaper," he said. "The editor has more or less given me a job. I'm going to borrow a typewriter. He's paying me twelve cents a line. There's no one else writing for the paper from around here."

"But there's nothing to write about in Avabäck," said Eva.

"You wait and see!" said Manfred. "You just wait and see!"

And then in the end they had to say a few words about the past after all.

"That schoolteacher who was lodging here the last time I was home, things went pretty fast for him."

"Yes. Things went fast."

"I saw him at Hällnäs just the once. In the library. He was asking for *Pilgrim's Progress*. But then he disappeared."

"Yes. He disappeared."

AND BERTIL, WHO is still alive, even if it's an increasingly wretched and less symmetrical life, also belongs to the unwritten. The Council must have taken care of him, of course, but that doesn't mean that his story is finished.

And Matilda Holmström, who no longer lives in Adakgruvan. Does the Council know about that?

Not to mention all the remaining stock in Robert Maser's bus. That ought to be recorded too, down to the last little shirt button and elastic band and handkerchief trimming.

And how will things go for Ellen in Lillsjöliden, how will her situation develop? It's very possible that Lars Högström the schoolteacher managed to transmit some extremely peculiar characteristics to her! What will the Council write about that?

And also: what is going to happen next in Lillåberg and Morken and Inreliden and Kullmyrliden and Brännberg and Lakaberg and Lillholmträsk?

And after that? When that too has happened and been recorded?

And so on and so forth.

I don't know.

BUT FINALLY, AT long, long last, Linda came back to him after all. She had a little birch bark box in her hand.

30

HE WAS PROPPED up on his pillow, wiggling one of his front teeth that was no longer completely firm. It was a way of passing the time. He preferred the loose tooth to the occupational therapy in the basement.

"Why did you desert me?" he asked.

"I've never deserted you," she said. "I've been on leave. Though now of course I've resigned."

She was wearing bright white dungarees tightly belted around the waist. Her hair had turned black since he had last seen her.

He sat up. "So you're abandoning me again," he said.

"I'll never abandon you," she replied. And he asked, "What season is it?"

"Don't you ever look out of the window?"

"Why should I look out of the window?"

"Winter," she said. "It's winter. One of our four winters."

She sat down beside him. She smelled of snow and wind

and cold but simultaneously of warmth. The Boston Symphony Orchestra was playing Liszt's *Dante Symphony* on his radio, a crackly and melancholy sound.

"Have you lost your hair?" she asked. "Isn't it growing any more?"

"I don't know," he said. "The Council shaves my head once a week."

"Do you see what this is?" she asked, proffering the birch-bark box.

"It's a birch bark box," he said. "Before the Council took my snuff away, I used to keep it in a box like that."

"Ah, yes," said Linda, "I remember."

They sat in silence for a while. Then she told him to open the box.

It contained a large lump of something reddish-gold and gleaming.

"No," he said, "I've never seen anything like that before."

"Haven't you read anything about it in the newspaper?"

No, why should he read the newspaper?

"It's gold."

"Fool's gold?"

"No—real genuine true gold."

"I see," he said. "There's nothing very special about it."

Then he leaned closer to her, looked deep into her eyes and said, "They've taken my brandy away!"

"It'll be okay," she said. "Everything will be okay."

Now she just had to tell him about the gold. She had tried to find Avaberg mountain hundreds of times. She had gone on foot, she had taken a snow scooter, she had even borrowed a boat and tried to approach from the lake. She had had the green Geographical Survey map in her hands and the Ordnance Survey map and the yellow Survey map, she had used binoculars and she had forced herself to sit for hours at the planimeter in the Civil Engineer's Department. And she had found all the other mountains, even eskers and hillocks and knolls. But not Avaberg mountain.

Did he still remember, she asked, once drawing her a map on a big white roll of paper?

"Yes, I remember. With the colored crayons."

"That map," she said, "was a miracle! With that, all I had to do was walk straight to it!"

"Yes," he said. "I know. That's where I lived for the greater part of my life."

"Fancy your being able to remember all that!"

"Imagination is my memory," he said modestly.

AND ONCE SHE had found Avaberg mountain her difficulties were over. She arranged all the formalities in accordance with the law on mineral exploitation, and got approval from the National Mining Corporation and the concession from the Planning Department. And all the papers had been signed today with the mining company.

"That's good," he said. "So you're free this afternoon. We're having pork loaf."

"Avaberg mountain," she went on, "was one long unbroken seam of gold, one elongated 250-foot-high lump of pure gold."

"Yes," he said, "I think I knew that."

She was now, without a shadow of doubt, the richest person in Västerbotten, even north of the Ångermanälven river. The Boliden Company had never been as rich as she was. Nor the Forestry Commission or the MoDo paper company.

"So this is why you're abandoning me?"

No, certainly not, she would never abandon him. That was why she had come: in order never to abandon him.

"That was very considerate of you," he said.

He should get dressed now straight away, he must leave all this behind him, he should even forget the pork loaf. She would take care of him till the end of time! And first and foremost he would be able to drink and above all eat just what his heart most yearned for.

"Will there be brandy?"

"Yes, of course there's brandy."

And she helped him get up, she pulled off the Council's pale blue pajamas and dressed him in his dark suit with waistcoat and white shirt, and from the limousine she had waiting outside she fetched a wolfskin coat to put over his shoulders.

"I shall give you back your freedom and life and creativity," she said. "I owe you that much."

"Thank you," he said absent-mindedly. "Thanks, that's really good of you."

As they emerged her chauffeur opened the rear doors of the limousine for them. He was wearing a dark blue uniform and a cap with a shiny peak.

"What's this vehicle called?" the former writer asked.

"It's called a Bentley."

"And where's the producer gas tank?"

"There isn't any producer gas any more," she said. "Nearly all autos run on gasoline now."

When they had made themselves comfortable in the back seat and she had instructed the chauffeur where to go, she asked, "But how were you able to draw that map?"

"It was nothing," he said. "It was nothing at all. It was just exactly the same as constructing a sentence."